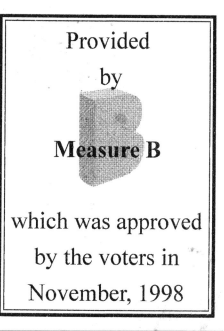

American Farmhouses
COUNTRY STYLE AND DESIGN

LEAH ROSCH

Principal Photography
KEITH SCOTT MORTON

A SMALLWOOD & STEWART BOOK

SIMON & SCHUSTER New York ★ London ★ Toronto ★ Sydney ★ Singapore

CONTENTS

Shaped by the Land ★ 12

America began as a nation of farmers and remained so for close to two hundred fifty years. From New England and Virginia westward, they created a rich heritage of vernacular architecture and design that continues to influence our homes today.

A Simplicity of Purpose ★ 20

An architectural survey of the most noteworthy farmhouse designs: Beginning with the log cabin, country builders developed their own uniquely American houses. Post-and-beam framing produced solid, highly practical styles such as the Cape Cod and saltbox. The invention of balloon frame construction set the stage for the more fanciful styles of the Victorian era.

The Soul of Ingenuity ★ 42

Practicality and resourcefulness were cornerstones of farmhouse life. This is evident in the interiors of their homes—the basis of what we know as "the country look." From stenciled walls to the corner cupboard to the fireplace, farmhouse interiors exhibit a style that is timeless and inspiring.

The Farmhouse Reclaimed ★ 58

Restoring a period farmhouse can be part research, part detective work, part historical imagination. The rooms in these homes show how the owners arrived at their distinctive looks:
Story-and-a-half Cottage, *Massachusetts* • Saltbox, *Connecticut* • Quaker-plan Colonial, *Pennsylvania* •

Few history books capture the story of America's past as vividly as the farmhouses that fill our countryside. These fundamentally practical homes chronicle the development of the nation, tracing both its expansion and growing prosperity. From the late 1600s to the late 1800s, pioneers in each new generation pushed ever westward from Massachusetts and Virginia, across the prairie to the plains of the Dakotas, until farmland ultimately yielded to the range. Mirroring the country's industrial progress, the architecture of their homes evolved from humble dwellings to the more elaborate styles that presided over the Victorian-era landscape.

For much of our history, we have been a nation of farmers, making the farmhouse our most prevalent form of architecture (if not our most celebrated or best documented). Beginning with the earliest settlers who farmed to feed their families, working the land was a primary occupation through most of the nineteenth century, when farming accounted for more than half of the gross national product. Even as recently as the early twentieth century, more than a third of the population was still involved in agriculture.

Owning land was—and still is—an essential part of the American Dream. It has always represented freedom, autonomy, an opportunity to make one's own way in the world—desires that had a particular resonance for the millions of immigrants who came

Shaped by

to these shores. For a young and growing nation, such dreams proved mutually beneficial. Fertile land, and plenty of it, was perhaps the greatest tangible asset this country had to offer. It shaped our history, our development, even our values. By the nineteenth

THE LAND

century, land had become the currency of expansion as the government offered millions of acres in exchange for the settling and cultivation of the burgeoning frontier. Aiding the effort was the advancement of the railroad, which made farming in even the most remote areas appealing as well as profitable.

At the heart of all farm life was the farmhouse. An inseparable part of the workplace, it was required to be multifunctional and ever versatile. This was where all family activities occurred and many chores were carried out. It showed its formal side in the front public rooms, while the hard-working kitchen, buttery, and pantry in the back were strictly utilitarian. And since farms generally remained in the same family for generations—mobility wasn't a consideration for those who made their living from their land—the farmhouse needed to be infinitely accommodating. As families grew, so did the house: A two-room structure would become a three-room dwelling, saltbox-style, with a lean-to grafted on its back; a one-room stone cottage could develop into a two-story farmhouse. When children married, it wasn't uncommon for entire wings to be added in order to provide them with their own first home.

At the same time, farmhouses were often updated to reflect prevailing tastes and construction improvements. Typically, in the eighteenth century, larger-paned windows replaced their multipaned predecessors and a more fashionable entryway was added—if only a paneled door and glazed transom. Sometimes, these enhancements were even more substantive: Over time, the same house might acquire a Federal-style doorway with an elliptical fanlight, a Greek Revival portico, and later still a Victorian-era bay window and fancy gingerbread details—producing some unusual architectural hybrids.

It is this mutable quality that helps explain why farmhouses defy easy classification, neat and tidy style labels, or even accurate dating. Comprised of architectural inconsistencies and floor-plan changes from multiple remodelings over the years, they are rarely, if ever, the same as they began.

American Farmhouses is a celebration of that singularity—an ode to the genre's practical and adaptive characteristics, its essential vernacular quality. It is not intended to be a comprehensive history of American rural architecture or a detailed region-by-region review (if such a book could even be compiled); instead, it offers an appreciative look at the beginnings of this most idiomatic architecture and design and explores some of the more notable expressions of its evolution.

Our primary objective in the opening pages was to identify types of farmhouses that have had an enduring architectural influence and remain relevant even today. Canvassing the country and selecting houses for inclusion was a daunting task, considering that there are nearly as many regional variations as there are regions. The shotgun, cracker, and octagon houses, for example, are all distinctive and intriguing, but survive more as historical curiosities; likewise, brick farmhouses are remarkable for their rarity.

By contrast, there are countless anonymous house types scattered across the country's farmland, as modest in pretension as they are in scale, which, while numerous, are of limited architectural interest. And while farmhouses, of course, do appear throughout the South, they seem to have been part of a separate and very different history: The tobacco- and cotton-fueled economy profoundly shaped the region's architecture, broadly dividing it into full-blown plantation houses or the most rudimentary sharecropper's shanties. Of certain noteworthy early Southern types, such as the French Colonial pavilion-roof cottage, precious few have survived.

"OUR FIELD IS THE WORLD."

LIGHT DRAFT. SUPERIOR DESIGN.

CLEAN AND RAPID CUTTER.

McCormick Harvesting Machine Co., Chicago.

ESTABLISHED 1831.

Most of the pages that follow are devoted to profiles of farmhouses as they are lived in today. Each house is accompanied by a date and a designation referring to when and in what form it was built (such as Cape Cod, Greek Revival, and so on). In several cases, the original architectural identity is still recognizable; in others, it's been erased as the house has evolved.

As with most contemporary farmhouses, these homes are no longer inhabited by people who work the land for a living. Still, they recall simpler times and less complicated pursuits. Built over a span of one hundred and fifty years, each has been thoughtfully and sensitively restored and refurbished. Some pay homage to their heritage, others display more artistic license in their design. Yet for all their diversity, they each provide a valuable connection to the past and a comfortable haven in the present.

Centuries before architect Louis Sullivan declared that form should follow function, this country's settlers were constructing farmhouses with practicality as their muse. Never to be confused with high style, farmhouse architecture was nonetheless rich with character, thanks to the varied design traditions their builders brought to these shores—from the earliest English and Dutch settlers to the French, Germans, and Scandinavians who followed. As carpenters and craftsmen became acclimated to their surroundings, Old World traditions yielded to New World conditions, and American farmhouse architecture was born.

In New England, wood was the favored material, and the sturdy post-and-beam frame dictated the use of basic shapes. To survive the winters, English colonists built houses around massive chimneys and with steeply sloping roofs. In the South, settlers developed house plans and porches to maximize air circulation. The Dutch left their mark with the gambrel roof and stone farmhouses in New York and New Jersey, while the Swedes introduced the log cabin to the Delaware Valley—a form that was so practical in this densely wooded country, it was adopted and adapted by virtually every other ethnic group in every other region for the next two hundred years. Even after the advent of mass-produced building materials, farmhouses retained their vernacular spirit—continuing to bring a strong regional and practical interpretation to formal architectural styles.

A SIMPLICITY

For all the differences in outward appearance, however, American farmhouses share a common thread of simplicity. This is architecture that epitomizes the integrity of basic forms and humble materials—making it accessible, timeless, and infinitely inspiring.

OF PURPOSE

SENTIMENTAL ICON

Long before its plucky Little House on the Prairie days, the log cabin was a favorite of Colonial pioneers—and for good reason. The earliest shelter (not counting sod homes, which were intended as temporary housing), it required only an ax and the trees felled to clear the land. No frame was necessary, not even sheathing: Round and notched logs would lock into place simply by their own weight, and the wood provided natural insulation.

The South has a long and innovative history of log buildings—two of the more common were the saddlebag and the dogtrot. The former had single rooms on either side of a central chimney (like a pair of saddlebags); by contrast, the dogtrot had an open hallway, or breezeway, separating two rooms. But it was the northern Europeans, settling mainly in parts of Wisconsin, Missouri, and Texas in the nineteenth century, who took log construction to new heights.

Expanding on the one- and two-room dwellings, Norwegians re-created their traditional farmhouses, built of square-hewn logs (opposite, top)—far more civilized with a second story and a porch. The lapped siding on the second-story gable was adapted from homegrown-American building methods. Finnish immigrants preferred a construction of loose-fitting round logs (opposite, bottom left) chinked with mortar.

Typically, logs were chinked with mud plaster, but other styles developed. Perhaps the most decorative is stovewood construction (above), so called because it used logs short enough to fit in a stove. The wood was set with limestone cement, cut ends out.

Germans introduced *fachwerk*, a construction style in which a framework of squared timbers was filled in with bricks (opposite, bottom right). In the East, it was soon replaced with post-and-beam framing; later immigrants brought it to the Midwest in the mid 1800s.

Little House, Big Ideas

With roots reaching almost as far back as Plymouth Rock and a pragmatic efficiency that prevailed well into the nineteenth century, the Cape Cod house (opposite) is so traditionally American that it could be the architectural equivalent of mom and apple pie. The model for much of postwar American housing, it's often what we think of when we think "home."

Designed to weather the harsh New England climate, Capes were built broad and close to the ground and were often situated to the south to take full advantage of the sun. Like many early wood-frame homes, they were of post-and-beam construction—a box-like system of house framing in which heavy timber posts were held in place by massive horizontal timber beams.

Steeply pitched gable roofs on the Cape Cod deflected the wind and shed the rain and snow. An enormous central chimney anchored the house and served all the fireplaces, of which there were usually four: one in each front parlor, in the kitchen, and in one of the two bedrooms upstairs. Cozy and unassuming, the Cape had a simple, symmetrical facade: two pairs of windows flanking a center door—the perfect punctuation to such a rational design.

Of equally straightforward style was the stone farmhouse (right) that figured in the Dutch-settled colonies of New York's Hudson River Valley and northern New Jersey. Such sensible forms, they were built with materials literally found in their own backyard: stones cleared from surrounding fields and mortar made of area limestone and ground shells. Small but mighty, they were also favored by the Germans and Scots-Irish who immigrated to Maryland and southern Pennsylvania in the early eighteenth century.

THE SENSIBLE SOLUTION

It's not exactly graceful. In fact, with its one overly elongated roofline, the saltbox house looks like a mistake. It proves that looks aren't everything, as this architectural oddity was the colonists' answer to overcrowding.

As families outgrew their one- and two-room homes, the quickest means of expansion was a single-story lean-to (which usually housed a kitchen, pantry, and birthing room) across the back. The result resembled a box used to store salt in medieval times, hence the name. In the South, the style was called a "catslide," the same moniker used by the English, from whom the settlers copied the concept.

One of the most popular candidates for the transformation was New England's garrison house (below), characterized by its jetty (the second-story overhang), decorative corner pendants, and projecting gable end. So successful was the expansion layout that by the 1680s, builders were incorporating the lean-to into original construction—and the classic saltbox was born (opposite). Though hardly sleek, the rear roofline lost its patchwork profile, and the chimney, which had gained a flue for the added kitchen's fireplace, was back to its normal, if still large, size.

A Fond Attachment

The connected farm was perhaps a phenomenon more than a type—and a highly regional one at that. Borrowed from a centuries-old English tradition of centralizing the compound, the plan first appeared in Maine in the early 1800s. The telescoping arrangement generally consisted of four buildings (and sometimes more): farmhouse, work kitchen, some kind of stable or work shed, and barn.

At first glance, its appeal would seem to be the convenience of the connected arrangement during inclement weather. But this does not explain why the configuration failed to spread to other northern regions of the country. Instead, it's thought that the proximity of the buildings were more efficient for the New England farmer who often also operated a home industry— such as tanning, metalworking, or carpentry—housed in the building adjacent to the barn. In the Midwest, where farming alone provided enough of a livelihood, such diversification was unnecessary.

Continuing for nearly a century, the connected-farm concept did travel to other parts of northern New England, but never beyond. By far its biggest constituency would be the progressive farmers of Maine, where many of these stately farmsteads can still be found.

THE NEW NATION'S NEW LOOK

Greek Revival, one of the most elegant architectural styles, seduced the nation for much of the mid 1800s. Originally known as the "National Style," it caught the country's post-Revolution mood by alluding to the democratic ideals of ancient Greece (a nation that was fighting its own war of independence in the 1820s).

From state capitols to banks, Greek Revival became the architecture of choice for most important institutions. Country builders also embraced the new mode, assisted in no small part by the highly popular pattern books of Asher Benjamin and others.

Building in the Neoclassical style was a sure sign of prosperity. Yet plenty of existing farmhouses were modified to feature Greek Revival details, creating some unusual hybrids. There are even a few examples of Colonial farmhouses being resited—literally picked up and turned ninety degrees in order to have the gable end facing forward—before getting a facelift.

Country carpenters remained enthralled with Greek Revival well after the rest of the nation moved on. In fact, the signature farmhouse style of a gabled front with pedimented windows (top right) continued into the twentieth century, as did the gable-front-and-wing design (opposite). But in classic vernacular fashion, there were many local interpretations of the style—such as cobblestone farmhouses (bottom right) found from Vermont to northern Illinois and Wisconsin.

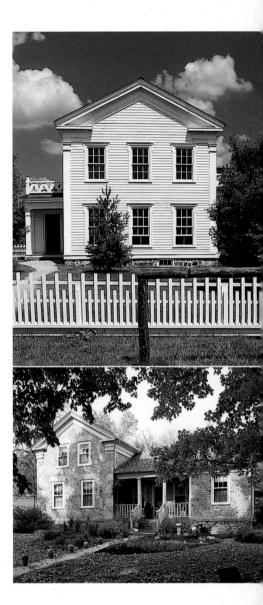

SOUTHERN COMFORT

As architectural forms go, the porch might not seem like much. But on a sultry summer day, even the simplest construction can feel inspired.

Exactly when porches debuted in this country is unclear; they're presumed to date to the French settlement of the Mississippi Valley and Gulf Coast, and be patterned after Caribbean plantation houses (viewed on trading expeditions to the islands). What is clear is that porches became a central fixture in Southern architecture and culture, vernacular and otherwise.

Over its history, the porch has had many permutations and a variety of names, such as gallery, piazza, and veranda. It was often the most prominent feature of a house. Even in the more humble cottage examples (above) that proliferated throughout the Deep South, the porch occupied a third of the square footage. The two-tiered gallery (opposite), as it was known, which can be traced to the French Colonial influence in Louisiana, Mississippi, and Missouri, offered both air conditioning and embellishment.

FREEDOM OF EXPRESSION

Balloon framing, a radically new construction method believed to have originated in the 1830s, changed the face of American architecture. The new system employed closely spaced wall studs that extended the full height of the frame. It also used standard-cut lumber and machine-made nails, which made post-and-beam's massive timbers and tedious joinery archaic by comparison. Together with the use of mass-produced components (windows, doors, roofing), which were becoming more widely available, balloon-frame construction transformed house building into a much simpler, faster, and less expensive process.

Leading the way for vernacular construction were Andrew Jackson Downing's hugely popular plan books, *Cottage Residences* (1842) and *The Architecture of Country Houses* (1850). His practical illustrated treatises made it possible for country craftsmen to emulate the reigning fashions of the day which ultimately fostered a profusion of ornamental styles that came to be known as Victorian. Farmers had their favorites, among them the gingerbread-rich Carpenter Gothic; the romantic Italianate (opposite); **Eastlake Style** (above), marked by highly decorative porches; and the fanciful and eclectic Queen Anne.

FOR A GRACIOUS AGE

In the second half of the nineteenth century, the beauty of America's industrial revolution was on display throughout the countryside. Victorian-style farmhouses, even the most modest, were exuberant reflections of the country's progress and prosperity.

The front porch was popularized with Victorian architecture, and farmhouses wore them well. Here was a place for the family to gather at day's end, to take stock, observe nature, and watch the world go by. The porch was also a place for individual expression, even with mass-produced materials. Farmers showed a fondness for decorative details that were now being turned out by steam-powered scroll saws. Yet, ever practical and unshowy, they tended to add judiciously (opposite, clockwise from top): gable accents and fish scale-shingles, sheltered by cornices; brackets placed beneath the eaves and bay windows; and fanciful trim and railings, covered by a porch roof.

On a farmhouse, the generous wraparound porch (above), a Queen Anne staple, could still feel low-key. Mixing elements of different fashions—such as these prominent Eastlake-style turned porch posts and Italianate bay window—somehow kept the house unassuming and less formal.

CHARACTER BUILDING

The barn, which debuted in the 1700s, has always held a central place in the rural American landscape. Early examples were patterned after the grain store-houses of Europe, which date to the Middle Ages when churches were among the most prominent buildings. Those early warehouses needed to be similarly spacious—which may explain why the soaring ceilings of American barns have something of a churchlike quality.

Like the first houses, barns were retooled to suit regional Colonial conditions. When painting was discovered to be a worthy wood preservative, Northern farmers used their most available ingredients—a mix of iron oxide and cows' milk—which gave rise to the great American tradition of red barns and other outbuildings (left).

Another early-American tradition was the barn raising (above), in which neighbors turned out to help erect the heavy timber frame, under the direction of a master barn builder. Raising the formidable post-and-beam structure required quite a collaborative effort—and the old barns that still populate our landscape speak of this community spirit.

THE MANY FACES OF THE AMERICAN BARN

The architecture of barns seems to have demanded nearly as much attention as that of the farmhouse itself. Probably because barns were less susceptible to changing architectural tastes, many old examples dotting the countryside still display early ethnic and regional characteristics.

One of the most distinctive is the gambrel roof (opposite, top left) which, judging by the number that still exist today, was quite a favorite for barns. Farmers appreciated the additional space provided above the rafters. Though the Dutch are credited with popularizing the design, it is believed to have been based on a medieval-English form. Built sometimes with flared eaves, sometimes with one sloping side, the gambrel roof appears in many variations and even more regions, evidence of its practicality.

The bank barn (opposite, bottom), which probably originated with the Pennsylvania Germans, was one of the more ingenious concessions to the terrain. Built into a slope, it housed livestock on the lower level, insulated by the ground; the upper floor typically stored the grain and feed. Accessed by different doors,

the split-story arrangement turned tricky terrain into a farmer's advantage.

Barn builders also had to consider the purpose of the outbuilding, which gave rise to an abundance of styles. Dairy cows, for example, needed different accommodations than did storing grain or drying tobacco leaves. Often, too, a hastily built structure was used as a transitional barn (opposite, top right) until the farmer had the means (or time) to erect something more substantial, at which point this temporary barn, rather than being razed, would be put to some other use.

Barn design would change and improve as farmers shared ideas and solutions. Then came the Industrial Revolution, and these outbuildings benefited from such progressive, and diverse, inventions as balloon-frame construction and the airtight grain silo. More than a hundred years earlier, however, experimentation produced the prototype for the round barn (left). The most famous example was built in 1826 in the Shaker Village of Hancock, Massachusetts, but George Washington is said to have developed one thirty years prior. While lauded for its efficiency, the round barn never caught on, though the occasional example continued to be built even into the twentieth century.

THE SOUL

Even in their most basic form, early farmhouses reflected their owners' optimism. They might have been small and built only with rudimentary materials, yet care was taken to construct everything on the square, the easier to build onto. And that care extended even to the most humble interiors and furnishings. These settlers were putting down roots.

Many First Period houses (New England historians' shorthand for those built between 1625 and 1725) started as one room, the hall, with a like-size sleeping chamber above. The room was all-purpose, its imposing hearth a lifeline. With any luck, after some decades, the one-room dwelling would be expanded with a similar layout of slightly smaller scale, creating the common hall-and-parlor plan. With further prosperity might come a more gracious, yet still cozy, four-room plan: two front parlors (the best and the common, serving as their names imply), the keeping room, and a kitchen. The best parlor doubled as the master bedroom by night, and on special occasions, the formal dining room; the keeping room, an upgrade from the versatile hall and a precursor to our living room, also served as the family dining room and, if needed, another bedroom. The upper story, whether half or full size, continued as sleeping quarters, including a crawl space for storage.

Expansion wasn't the only sign of advancement; windows could be very revealing. Natural light was a luxury in early houses—glass of any size was expensive and conse-

OF INGENUITY

quently, window placement an art. As glassmaking and construction techniques improved in the eighteenth century, diamond-paned casement windows gave way to twelve-over-twelve lights in a sliding sash (twelve panes of glass in top and bottom). Before century's end, these were succeeded by nine-over-nine and various other configurations of still fewer and larger lights, or panes, as windows assumed more aesthetic significance.

To compensate for the lack of interior lighting, families relied on candles, which, like so many other necessities of eighteenth-century life, were made on the farm. As with so many utilitarian items, they inspired a decorative form in the wall sconces and candlesticks that still influence modern-day designs. In fact, from blanket chests to baskets, the roots of much of American folk art can be traced to the farmhouse. This was a world in which most everything that was needed had to be made by hand. Compelled by necessity, with a mandate for economy, farmwives created rag rugs and patchwork quilts from fabric scraps, stitched coverlets and samplers from homespun yarn—and in the process, spawned a uniquely American design heritage that is still treasured today.

With the industrial transformations of the nineteenth century, home life on the farm changed as profoundly, if not as rapidly, as did urban life. Breakthroughs in construction and materials allowed for bigger houses, with more (and more spacious) rooms; cookstoves and later, running water, revolutionized kitchen duties; the hand-turned sewing machine simplified making and mending clothes; and a little thing called the Mason jar had a huge impact on preserving fruits and vegetables.

Yet, long after the railroad and mail-order catalogs brought all manner of factory-made goods to the most distant rural outposts, farm families continued to do some things the old-fashioned way. Amid the growing uniformity of mass production, they preserved the personal expression evident in the handmade and the homegrown. It is this basic beauty of the farmhouse ethic, and aesthetic, that keeps us connected to a rich past and gives us a familiar place to come home to.

Hearth and Home

As with most farmhouse icons, the fireplace existed first for necessity. In the Northeast, where heat was nearly as vital as food, most early Colonial farmhouses were built around an enormous central chimney. Accompanying fireplaces were equally sizable, with the cooking fireplace—the *only* fireplace in two- and three-room plans—the largest. The open brick hearth, often big enough to walk into, was designed with a bake oven at its back. Later, the bake oven was moved alongside for convenience and given a separate flue.

In warmer climes, chimneys and fireplaces were built into end gables or even the exterior of the house in an effort to avoid overheating. For the same reason, the summer kitchen, a nearby outbuilding with a large cooking fireplace, became common in the South and on prosperous New England farmsteads.

As chimney construction became more sophisticated in the 1700s, flues were used to support individual fireplaces. Those in the public rooms could now be built smaller, unleashing their decorative potential. The mantel, which started simply as convex molding framing the opening, was soon topped with a shelf. Before century's end, the Rumford fireplace—an innovative design that reflected more heat into the room and lessened the amount of smoke—had become common, as had carved mantelpieces, however primitive.

With the introduction of the Franklin stove, an efficient cast-iron appliance for heating and cooking, fireplaces were on the wane. By the late 1800s, wood- or coal-burning cookstoves had become the norm. Yet, if the fireplace was being made technically obsolete, the appeal of its cozy-hearth image would endure.

WALL TREATMENT

The rudimentary pine planks that sheathed farmhouse interiors were being upgraded in the public
rooms to paneling by the mid 1700s. First treated with
linseed oil, like most bare-wood surfaces, paneled walls
were soon painted to brighten the small, dark rooms.

Farmwives had already discovered the beauty of
painting baseboards black to hide dirt. For the walls,
color choices varied by region, determined as much by
local minerals suitable for concocting paint (brick red
was prevalent, courtesy of the iron-rich soil over much
of the countryside) as by the farmers' native background. German settlers, for instance, brought a colorful tradition, seen in the eighteenth-century interiors of
southeastern Pennsylvania—though few were as brilliant
as in the circa 1758 farmhouse of Peter Wentz
(opposite)—and more flamboyantly in the Victorian
farmhouses of the Midwest and Texas.

In many farmhouses of the South, two contrasting
shades were often used in the same room; similarly, in
parts of New England parlors were done in two bright
tones to compensate for the general lack of furniture.
Still, variations on brownish red, muddy ochre, and dark
green were among the reigning rural shades of the late
1700s, as well as a steely blue-gray. This color was so
popular (and tenacious) that it is almost always the last
coat uncovered when stripping paneling today.

By the nineteenth century, lath and plaster
replaced paneling, which was reduced to wainscot and
chair rails except on the few remaining fireplace walls
(and even there it was typically fashioned into a mantelpiece). Plaster, a mixture of lime and sand with animal
hair as a binder, was time-consuming to apply and
no guarantee against heat loss. Still, whitewashed and
with painted trim, plastered walls offered farmhouses
a more progressive look.

DECORATIVE PAINTING

Following the Revolution, in farmhouses from New England to the Mid-Atlantic states and into the South, elaborately stenciled walls became something of a rage. Largely the work of itinerant artists, stenciling as well as freehand painted designs were a more affordable alternative to the imported wallpapers that graced affluent homes.

No surface was off-limits, it seems. Even front-parlor floors were stenciled; by the mid nineteenth century, spatter-painted styles were seen. Sometimes, the pine floors were painted in a black-and-white checkerboard design, imitating the marble floors of Europe. Probably more common were heavy-canvas floorcloths, painted in the checkered design, and used to protect (and camouflage) worn areas, particularly in entry halls and on stairs. In the South, where painted floors were rare, floorcloths often filled the whole parlor.

Like marbling, which often accented fireplaces and sometimes even baseboards, graining was further evidence of early American ingenuity. Inexpensive woods were meticulously painted in the likeness of such elegant varieties as mahogany and rosewood. Interior doors were most commonly grained—achieving an impressive degree of realism—but window and door surrounds, mantels, even chair rails were also fitting prospects.

SPACE SAVERS

Built-in furniture remains proof of the Colonial farmer's instinct for efficiency at a time when free-standing storage pieces were both costly and hard to come by. Certainly a necessity in the pantry and buttery off the kitchen, they found their way into other rooms as well—first as open shelves behind paneled doors built into the fireplace wall, then as more stylish, yet still functional, display pieces. By the second half of the eighteenth century, built-ins had become a signature of early-American architecture—from the box bed of Dutch Colonial and German farmhouses, enclosed to conserve heat, to the ubiquitous corner cupboard, handsomely detailed and fit into a parlor's otherwise unused space.

Typically divided into upper open display case and lower storage cupboard, corner pieces were often framed in carved molding and featured folk designs such as scalloped detailing, derivative of the period's popular shell-head pattern. In the early 1800s, as glass became more affordable, the upper half of corner cabinets began to feature glazed doors.

Over time, the canny built-in cupboard gave way to floor-to-ceiling china closets, Victorian style, and later into niche-maximizing hanging cabinets in the kitchen. But perhaps its best legacy is the built-in closet—for which contemporary American society is indebted to the wiles of farmhouse construction.

STAIRCASE ASCENT

In early New England homes, space was tight
and the box staircase—literally boxed in between the
chimney and the parlor wall—was the solution. Never
mind that in these story-and-a-half houses, the ascent
could be dauntingly steep. Often, a staircase door
(opposite) was built in an effort to stave off drafts. The
box winder was a variation on this staircase; it also rose
alongside the chimney but had a right-angle pivot of
steps at the bottom and top. Although this winding
design managed to eke out a few more precious feet of
space, the climb remained steep.

As farmhouse architecture moved away from the
basic center-chimney design in the late 1700s, the staircase was liberated and became more of a decorative
feature. Many farmhouses began adopting staircases of
open-string construction—styles that revealed more
of their stair-ends, with a handrail supported by a newel
post and balusters. At first these components were
primitive and squared off, but they were soon replaced
with more elaborately turned and carved designs. Stair-
ends, too, became a decorative feature, as farmhouse
staircases took on the hallmark of fine furniture.

By the early 1800s, with the aid of pattern books,
curved flights were turning up in the more affluent
or newly-built farmhouses. Circular staircases appeared,
too, as more ornate styles began to inform the work
of country craftsmen.

Farmhouse & Garden

In addition to the large-scale crop growing that was the farmer's livelihood, vegetable and herb gardens were common to the eighteenth-century farm. Planted near the house for easy access, they were the model for today's kitchen gardens, yielding medicinal and household remedies as well as food. These home-lot gardens, as they called, loosely patterned after the medieval-English model, were enclosed by simple pale or picket fences as a means of protection from animals and the farm's own livestock.

By the end of the century, fenced-in parlor gardens, situated in front of the house, were popular. Roses and other perennials were planted there in neat rows, along with herbs and annuals. Parlor gardens continued to acquire more ornamental flowers and, by the mid 1800s, as a show of gentility, the front yards of progressive farmers acquired decorative picket fences. The Victorian era gave rise to an impressive array of patterns—guaranteeing that the white picket fence would always be entwined with the farmhouse ideal.

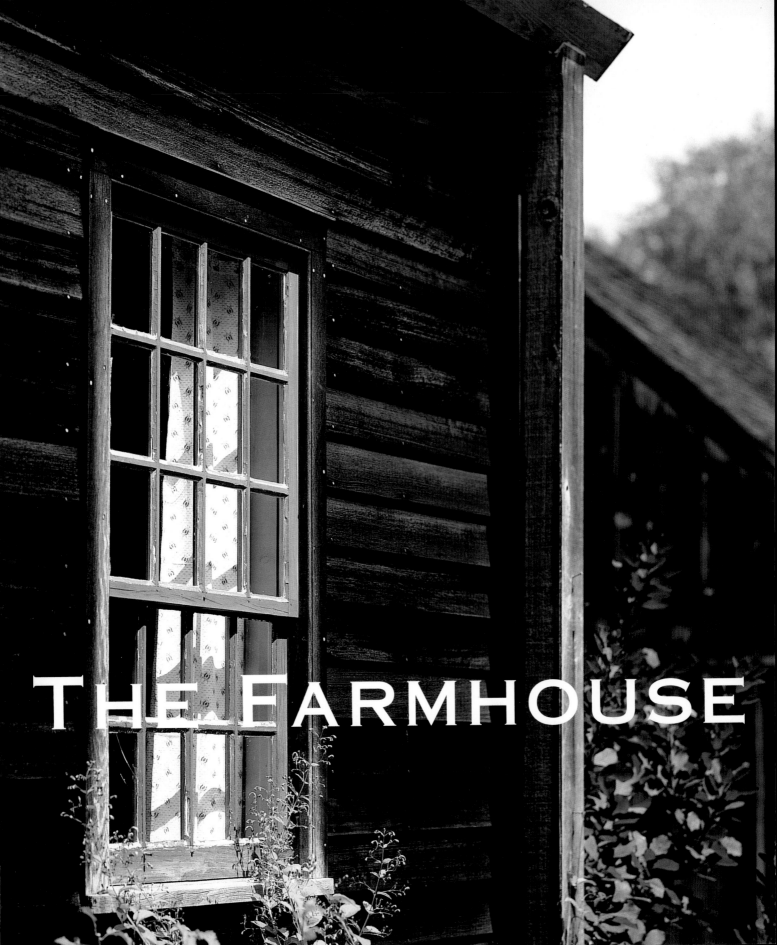

THE FARMHOUSE

We respond instinctively to a restored farmhouse. Perhaps it's the sense of history, a tangible reminder of our heritage. Or maybe it's the feel of authenticity—the wide floor-boards, multipaned windows, wainscot, moldings, clapboard, and other staples that in mass reproduction have become popularized—as well as homogenized—as "period style." Patina, after all, can't be manufactured.

There's also something extraordinary about historic farmhouses. They were built largely by hand, one at a time; and though they might have been patterned after common European forms or later, designs from plan books, they were generally adapted to the needs of their owners and environment. This is why we find saltbox styles only in the earliest colonies, for example, or shingled siding specifically in eastern New York where cedar was abundant. Today, in an age that encourages expediency and conformity over craftsmanship and individuality, the singularity of the farmhouse holds great appeal.

Equally compelling, old farmhouses tell stories of the life and times of the families who lived there, which is another reason why they're well worth preserving. They are wood and brick essays on America's evolution, imbued with the traditions and values that are still an essential part of our national fabric. They're also "roadside museums," reflecting far more accurately the way most people lived than do grand landmark-status mansions.

RECLAIMED

Yet unlike traditional museums, the best preservations are comfortable and lived-in, by design—with timeworn floors, faded finishes, and furnishings that show their age. In conserving these farmhouses, their owners provide a poignant window on our past.

WHILE HISTORY DOESN'T LIE, IT SURELY can mislead, as the owners of this First Period timber-framed house in Ipswich, Massachusetts, would attest. The oldest section of the now-fourteen-room farmhouse has been dated at 1638, early 1650s, and 1670. Now there's even a question whether historians have bestowed elder status on the wrong portion of the house altogether. Call it the contrary side of progress: The more advanced the technology for dating houses becomes, the less things are as they once seemed.

Yet, for the preservationist owners of the Merchant-Choate house, so named for two of its seventeenth-

THE HISTORY LESSON

century families, the discovery process has provided a unique look at three centuries of New England country life. The house is remarkable as one of the oldest survivors of Massachusetts Bay—though it's now difficult to envision its beginnings as a one-room "cottage" (in early parlance, a small, unassuming dwelling) with a massive chimney bay and a sleeping loft under a steeply pitched roof. In 1705, it was joined with another story-and-a-half house relocated from elsewhere in Ipswich, creating a two-over-two-room plan.

Contributions from nearly every generation and fashion enrich its fabric, an evolution that the owners have respectfully tried to retain in their conservation. That means that, from room to room, the mood can fluctuate whole centuries—from the Georgian formality of the living room to the Victorian feel of a later guest room, with its unpaneled walls, ornamental fireplace, and closets dating to the late 1800s. The owners have retained some timeworn features as well—namely exposed three-hundred-year-old timbers and a few dozen coats of peeling whitewash—because that kind of poetic authenticity cannot be captured by modern research.

★ Illustrative of the progression of this seventeenth-century farmhouse, the left side entrance (opposite) connects an early-twentieth-century addition (which includes a period six-over-nine window, reused from elsewhere in the house) with an addition from the late eighteenth century. The homeowner painted the entry-hall floor in Colonial checkerboard pattern. ★ Three hundred years of pottery shards and other signs of life found on the property (above) provide a glimpse into the home's past.

★ What now functions as a small dining room (opposite) was originally a kitchen, added to the house in the late 1700s. Its furnishings mostly share the earlier room's vintage: The transitional chair, one of a pair created by a mid-eighteenth-century craftsman in western Massachusetts, combines a characteristic Queen Anne-style carved splat and crest rail with William and Mary-style turnings. Accompanying it is a later-period tilt-top tea table in cherry from Connecticut. Sharing wall space above are a circa 1815 pastel of a Massachusetts sea captain and an exquisite presentation banjo clock from the mid 1800s. ★ In the living room (above), formerly the singular hall of the earlier cottage, furnishings range in origin from England to Hong Kong and in age from the 1690s to the 1960s. Rough whitewashed boards have given way to paneled beams and painted plaster walls. The brick fireplace lintel is a replacement for the original oak lintel, which, like so many of its era, not so surprisingly burned out.

★ Filtering through the nineteenth-century-updated windows (left), sunlight struggles to brighten the low-ceilinged dining room, which was formerly the original hall of the second cottage. Period furnishings enhance the room: An elegant American Classical mahogany dining table is paired with English Chippendale chairs, Chinese export porcelain peers over an exquisite William and Mary high chest bearing its original burled veneers and painted base, and vintage decanters and oil lamps gather on the McIntire-school swing-leg card table. Heavy upholstery fabric on the walls serves as both drapery and wallpaper—and insulation, for that matter. A twentieth-century oil painting of the homeowner's grandfather, the descendant of a founding family of Ipswich, is prominently displayed.

★ A nineteenth-century papier mâché moonface snuffbox (top right) offers an amusing complement to the painted top of an antique candlestand.

★ In the second-floor study (bottom right), a twisted brick chimney of mysterious purpose and design now serves as architectural sculpture. A jaunty contemporary mobile, enjoying the draftiness of the old house, finds itself forever in flight.

OF ALL THE CHARMS OF LIVING IN AN AUTHENTIC EIGHTEENTH-CENTURY house, having enough natural light and space are not usually among them. Neither, for that matter, is a reasonable-size kitchen. Consequently, after two decades of trying to overlook such shortcomings in his otherwise flawlessly restored Connecticut farmhouse—a pre–Revolutionary War saltbox with an 1830s L-shape addition—retired antiques dealer George Schoellkopf resolved to add on: not with new period-style construction, but a 20-by-50-foot, two-story-tall, modified-saltbox-style barn from a few miles away, whose vintage and bones were akin to the house.

Once a barn-restoration company had dismantled the structure (after numbering all its pieces), Schoellkopf and fine art photographer Gerald Incandela, with whom he shares the house, had it transported to their property and reassembled between the main house and an original hay barn. Several years into its

**Saltbox
circa 1770** # BUILDING ON THE PAST

new incarnation, the post-and-beam shell seamlessly houses the new kitchen and living room—a true "great room," light-filled and airy, with an 18-foot-high ceiling—and, on the lower level, an office and darkroom. With the exception of a pair of French doors overlooking a small, east-facing balcony, a few unobtrusively placed windows, the exterior brick cladding, and, okay, the plaster on the interior walls, everything is either original to the barn or authentic to the period.

That's because Schoellkopf, a passionate collector of American primitive antiques (with a knowledge of early-American history to match) is fundamentally a purist at heart. For all the painted farm furniture, hooked rugs, folk art, and vintage collections of slipware, redware, earthenware, and Delftware that decorate his home, hardly one was made outside Colonial New England. The result, then, is a harmoniously scaled four-bedroom farmhouse, with kitchen, living room, parlor, and basement, which lovingly wears a centuries-old patina and quietly satisfies contemporary creature comforts, all at the same time.

★ From the front, the saltbox (top right) looks much the same as when colonist Samuel Hollister built it in 1770. ★ The farmhouse remained in his family until the 1930s and gained several additions over the next two hundred years (bottom): an L-shape annex around 1830, twin dormers on the main house in the 1850s, and most recently, an old barn, which the current owners clad in brick and transformed into an open kitchen/living room. ★ An English-style boxwood garden (top left) bears all-white blooms in season.

★ The kitchen (opposite) features an assortment of eighteenth-century hanging cabinets still bearing their original Spanish-red paint and a one-hundred-year-old, 11-foot-long farmhouse table. The one witty incongruity: a trio of mid-nineteenth-century Chinese garden stools serving as table seating. ★ An antique apron-style marble sink (above) and countertops of polyurethaned old wood mix perfectly with the custom-made period-style cabinetry and window, a copy of the twelve-over-eight lights on the main house.

★ The pine paneling and mantel in the reconstituted barn (left) were acquired from another Connecticut house of the same vintage. Both decorative and functional, the seating includes a pair of Louis XVI armchairs, a sack-back Windsor, circa 1780, and a venerable late-seventeenth-century Carver armchair appointed with a flame-stitched cushion made from an eighteenth-century pattern book. From the same era, redware and slipware, once purely utilitarian, now add charm to the mantel. A primitive wooden horse, displayed on a painted, country Queen Anne side table was a child's toy. Replacing the original barn flooring, salvaged eighteenth-century oak planks are topped by an antique Kazak rug. ★ An eighteenth-century banister-back side chair (above) is remarkable for its unusually high seat, probably made for a ceremonial purpose. Overhead, the painted wooden checkerboard dates to about 1820.

★ The original keeping room (opposite), now used as a more formal living room and enhanced with a few favored folk antiques, shows its authentic two-hundred-year-old visage. The primitive portrait, like others in the house, is oil on canvas. The smoke-grained finish on the frame, a late-eighteenth-century folk art design, was created by scorching the wood with a candle and varnishing over the pattern. The consolelike table is a lift-top dough box dating to around 1810, when it was used as a place to store rising bread dough overnight. Painted in the period's ubiquitous Spanish red, it was then treated to the popular decorative-painting technique of graining. An exquisitely made reproduction Queen Anne wing chair is the room's lone imposter. ★ An antique pencil-post bed (above), graced with a canopy of two-hundred-year-old tape-trimmed linen, defines a private space within this guest room. An early-nineteenth-century linsey-woolsey quilt (so called for its presumed combination of linen and wool, though most were made of wool alone) supplies equal parts warmth and color. The wall of raised paneling, exhibiting remnants of its original blue-gray paint, came from a contemporary of this house.

IF MOST RESTORATIONS REQUIRE A CERTAIN AMOUNT OF DETECTIVE WORK to uncover the details of a home's original fabric, the job of piecing together the past of this Chester County, Pennsylvania, farmhouse could serve as a master class in Holmesian sleuthing.

Abandoned for nearly twenty-five years by the time Mark and Anna Myers took possession in 1989, the once proud Quaker farmstead had become prey to rough weather and rougher vandals. But the couple, who had already survived the restoration of one old house, had a sentimental incentive: The house was an heirloom, in Anna Myers's family since her grandfather, Edward Walton, a banker and dairy farmer, had purchased it in 1912; she is also a direct descendent of Thomas Woodward, one of the farm's original owners. With such ties, the couple wanted to honor its origins while making the house habitable—a proposition that would take architect Susan Maxman and a team of carpenters and stone masons five years.

BORN AGAIN

Quaker-plan
Colonial
circa 1760

Built in 1760 as a three-room dwelling, Pennock House (named for the family that lived there the longest) gained a stone summer kitchen at its back sometime before 1780. It more than doubled in size to a four-bay Georgian plan around 1806 with the addition of a brick-and-stone extension and a second floor. Since then, however, there had been no structural updates. So, in addition to providing basic necessities—namely, central heating, hot water, and twentieth-century wiring—the restoration included converting one of the five bedrooms into two guest baths and constructing two one-story glassed-in porches between the summer kitchen and the main house. One thing that could not be improved upon: the Franklin stove in the 1806 family room. Still fully functional, to say nothing of fuel efficient, the more than two-hundred-year-old invention clearly challenges the modern concept of built-in obsolescence.

★ From the front (opposite), this stately example of mid-eighteenth-century Quaker construction in Pennsylvania's Delaware Valley looks like an all-brick farmhouse. The unbracketed door hood and facing interlocked benches—a pared-down porch, Quaker style—were re-created from such centuries-old clues as weather scars on the brick and remnants of cantilevered joists. ★ From the back (above), the stone construction of the 1806 kitchen addition and more recent enhancements are visible.

★ The entrance hall was the keeping room in the initial three-room Quaker plan (which included two adjacent rooms, one for entertaining, the other for sleeping). Though spare on the exterior, the farmhouse features a selection of original interior moldings, a subtle sign of affluence. Accenting restored whitewashed walls, the brown and yellow-gold on the chair rail, baseboard, and staircase echo the earliest color scheme, determined after chips of the trim's old paint were professionally analyzed and matched to the closest color equivalents. Furnishings are a mix of family pieces and purchased antiques, all suited to the farmhouse period. The high chest, typical of late-eighteenth-century Chester County case pieces, would traditionally have held such a public spot. A Chippendale-style mirror graces the wall above a vintage, drop-leaf cherry dining table. Anchoring the opposite wall is a Hepplewhite card table. The only indication of modern times is a cast-iron radiator, unobtrusively installed by the current owners—the first to equip the house with heat.

★ Restoring the original front parlor (opposite), now used as the formal living room, was something of a treasure hunt. The mantel on the corner fireplace had been removed—by looters, it turns out (apprehended before they could make off with the goods)—and stored in a neighboring barn. The giveaway that it belonged to this fireplace was its hand-carved dentil molding, a perfect match to that of the room's built-in corner cupboard. Careful stripping of the fireplace's painted slip revealed the original marbleized finish. In keeping with the room's formality—as well as its tiny 12-by-12-foot scale—damask-covered Queen Anne–style wing chairs hobnob with a pair of Chippendale-style armchairs around a late-eighteenth-century tilt-top tea table. ★ Working from a local historian's slides of the room in its better days, a cabinetmaker was able to replicate the missing doors on the corner cupboard (top right)—lost in a successful heist, no doubt. The rich red interior is reminiscent of the circa 1760 shade. ★ Directly across the hall is the larger family room (bottom right), part of the later addition. It boasts the original Franklin stove, standing in for a fireplace.

TRADITION DIES HARD IN PARTS OF CONNECTICUT where families have lived for generations, some since the earliest settlers. Here, oral history can take precedence over the present, no matter how outdated the facts. That explains why this small clapboard saltbox in Warren is still called "Mrs. Carey's house"—even though the late Mrs. Carey last lived there in 1970, and the farmhouse has gained two antique annexes since 1976, a year after art historian and writer May Brawley Hill and her art-dealer husband, Frederick, bought it.

Though the house had been in Mrs. Carey's family for some fifty years (she inherited it from her parents), neither they nor their predecessors had thought to alter it much.

GUIDED BY TRADITION

Saltbox
circa 1738

This was fortunate for the preservation-minded Hills, since it meant inheriting a classic saltbox plan of three tiny rooms downstairs, two above; pine floors and stairs graciously worn by time; three fireplaces supported by the original central chimney; and twelve judiciously placed nine-over-six windows on the first floor.

Both in restoring the house and in adding on to it, the couple was careful to maintain its essential character—from searching out the rosehead nails that adorn the board-and-batten front door to relocating an old barn in which to house a new kitchen and family room. As more space was needed, they acquired another local eighteenth-century structure, a two-room house about to be razed, to serve as a guest room and the family dining room. Furnishings, too, are true to the farmhouse's roots—especially in the case of a dropleaf table in the old kitchen, thought to be original to the house. Found by Jeffrey Morgan, an historic-interiors consultant well versed in the local lore, it still bears an age-stained cloth embroidered with the initials of Ebenezer Marsh, for whom the home was built. It's this kind of tradition that now warmly informs Mrs. Carey's house. Surely, she would approve.

★Seen from the back of its second addition (opposite), the homestead, with its weathered quarter-sawn oak clapboard and enclosed porch made from salvaged wood, looks remarkably like any Colonial farmhouse enlarged over time. ★ The post-and-rail fence (above), with its strap-hinged, closed-picket gate, though period in feeling, is a late-twentieth-century arrival.

★ The granite-block hearth (above), graced with an iron fireback, warms the old kitchen, now a library for the homeowner's American art books. An eighteenth-century settle, draped with an old homespun blanket, evokes the room's modest heritage. ★ The fireplace in the barn annex's family room (opposite) came from the two-room-house addition. The 'N' on the stone chimney, built when the fireplace was moved, is for the Hills' son, Nathaniel. Windows in both added structures were enlarged to capture more light.

★ Period furnishings (opposite)—a gateleg table, early Windsor rod-back dining chairs, and one of a pair of stately William and Mary chairs—enrich the parlor, the oldest room in the house. Following scars on the wall, the owners moved the corner cupboard from the adjacent room to its rightful place, where it displays export china and creamware. ★As the stairs and beaded paneling (above) each had early traces of both blue and red paint, the owners took an equal-opportunity approach in employing the historical colors.

WITH HOUSES, AS WITH LIFE, THERE'S A KNACK TO KNOWING WHEN TO leave well enough alone. Fortunately, for this elegant farmhouse at the eastern end of Long Island, its earlier owners have mostly shared this sentiment. So when architectural designer Richard Lear and his landscape-designer wife, Elizabeth, purchased the place in 1986, it still possessed nearly all of its pre–Revolutionary War integrity and charms. Some more visible than others, it turned out.

A classic East Coast Colonial with Federal-style trimmings, the house began life in the late eighteenth century as a modest Cape Cod. It was built for Samuel Sherrill, a barrister from New England who was an early settler of the one-time potato-farming and fishing village, and it remained in his family's hands until 1956. During its first seventy-five years, the farmhouse grew into a saltbox with the addition of a lean-to at the rear of the house, and then into a full two-story dwelling. A back ell was added in 1885 to accommo-

AMERICAN BEAUTY

Cape Cod
circa 1770

date a dining room, additional bedrooms, and an updated kitchen—thereby relieving the keeping room, with its sizable fireplace and beehive oven, of its cooking duties.

For the Lears, removing all the drywall, a 1950s "improvement," was a must. They were intent on uncovering the original pine paneling throughout the house. Little did they realize that eliminating the drywall was only the first step; they next had to relieve the paneling of nearly two centuries' worth of paint. The couple painstakingly stripped away layers and layers to reveal the walls' original finish—a wonderful charcoal-green milk paint in remarkably good shape, which they preserved by first oiling, then waxing.

In the master bedroom they uncovered an intact working fireplace, one of four in the house all supported by the original center chimney. Apparently, the previous owners had boarded it up to fabricate an unbroken stretch of wall for their two single beds—further evidence that the mid twentieth century was clearly not this farmhouse's most flattering design period.

★ Graced by pilasters and an elliptical fanlight, the entrance is a classic example of Federal style, known for distinctive doorways on otherwise restrained façades. Yet, if judicious in elaboration, the entryway is long on ingenuity—evidenced by the unusual split door, no doubt an early form of heat conservation. Its two-thirds width was employed for ordinary comings and goings; for wider passage, the extra third opens. The original 36-inch cypress-shingle siding is typical of the area's early farmhouses.

★ With its milk-painted paneled walls, wide plank flooring, and sizable cooking fireplace, the great room (left), as the owners now employ what was originally the kitchen, appears to have been barely touched by time. Adding to the effect, a mural on the chimney breast depicts the village as it might have looked when the house was built. Pillows of vintage toile de Jouy lend patina to slipcovered furnishings; a gilded Chippendale-style mirror and eighteenth-century japanned chest, both found in the attic, provide an elegant touch. ★ A trio of vessels (above left), unified by their copper luster, lines up on the front parlor mantel. ★ In the nineteenth-century addition, the dining room (above right) hosts eight Windsor chairs and an English tavern table. ★ The central staircase (right) is a late-Colonial classic, with simple, square balusters and open stair-ends. An exuberantly painted period chest enlivens the nook.

★ Well-preserved late-eighteenth-century wallpaper (opposite) was the reward for the tedious task of stripping the stairwell. A drop-leaf table with burled-maple veneer and cherry legs adds period character, as does the graceful valance. While not original, the late-nineteenth-century window still boasts old glass. ★ White cotton bedding, curtains, and cutwork dust ruffles (above) cozy up the daughters' bedroom. In a nod to the decorative arts of the era, the homeowner comb-painted the door panels.

★ The two-story Federal farmhouse (right) cuts a proud profile. Enhanced by a white picket fence with beveled post caps
(a loving reproduction of one that surrounded the house in the
early nineteenth century), it's no wonder visitors to town often
mistake the home for an historic museum. ★ Several original
roof boards in the attic (above) bear builder's notes from more
than a hundred fifty years ago. Still legible, they document
prodigious lumber orders and construction notes.

AT FIRST GLANCE, THERE'S LITTLE TO SUGGEST THAT THIS PICTURESQUE farm, situated on 25 acres in rural Patterson, New York, is anything but a traditional connected farmstead. Looks can be deceiving. In fact, five of the interconnected buildings were added to the original 1740s story-and-a-half saltbox in the late 1980s. The design, by architect McKee Patterson, skillfully adapts the modest scale of an historic home to present-day living. Proof that the best ideas are timeless, the approach borrows from the typical expansion of nineteenth-century northern New England farms—an L-shape plan connecting the farmhouse with the "barn," which here serves as the great room.

Not much is known of the farm's past. The saltbox is thought to have originally been lived in by sharecroppers who worked the surrounding blueberry and apple orchards. Today, its lean-to removed,

**Saltbox
circa 1740**

THE LITTLE HOUSE THAT GREW

it contains the living room, dining room, and two upstairs guest bedrooms and baths. Additional living quarters flank the main house: to the left, the master bedroom suite and tin-roofed terrace; to the right, a passageway that links the dining room with the kitchen, above which are three children's bedrooms.

Great pains were taken to breathe old life into the new interiors. Wide floorboards match old-growth originals, with look-alike antique white oak filling in for the less available chestnut. Window frames copy those in the saltbox, with the number of lights updated to mimic later additions. High transom windows recall ones in Vermont's bygone sugar houses, doors sport old-time iron hardware, and a whitewashed framed ceiling tops the kitchen. In the original house, the work was mostly restorative (after first removing the aluminum siding and a few other "modern" remodeling touches): opening up plastered-over fireboxes, replacing worn floorboards, re-creating moldings and mantels. And although the house was wired for electricity, the dining room stays true to its era and is lit only by candles.

★ Echoing connected-farm architecture, late-twentieth-century additions blend seamlessly with the mid-eighteenth-century farmhouse at their center (opposite, bottom). Pine clapboard, "weathered" with bleaching oil, cloaks all the exterior walls; in a reference to its architectural inspiration, it runs vertically on the barnlike annex. ★ The original back of the house (top left) is now the front. ★ A window was sacrificed for the new entryway (top right), which opens onto a small parlor.

★ Waxed pine panels line the walls of the "seed room" (above), so called for its stash of gardening books. The new four-panel door leading to the stone terrace was whitewashed and distressed to achieve its period look. ★ In front of the impressive fireplace in the original kitchen, now the dining room (right), Hitchcock chairs add formality to an odd pairing of furnishings: a primitive, cypress-top table from the homeowner's native state of Texas and a New England barn-siding table of similar vintage. On the pine mantel, vintage pewter flanks an early-American chocolate mold.

★Originally the front staircase, this steep flight (opposite), built around the original center chimney, leads to a pair of guest bedrooms. The boxed-in design, high risers, and narrow treads are typical of early stairwells. ★ In the smaller guest room (above and right), stenciling by decorative artist Virginia Teichner takes its inspiration and color palette from early-American designs. Pocket shutters, reminiscent of Colonial window coverings, dress the tiny portals under the eaves; a Sheraton writing table, twin tin sconces, and a painted farmer's pail are congenial accoutrements.

★ The kitchen (opposite) is a study in historic charm and contemporary comforts: Punched-tin cabinet panels (the motif is an ode to the owner's Texas roots) complement the modern commercial range; Vermont slate paves the countertops and determined the Colonial shade for the milk-painted cabinetry. ★ The "shed room" (above)—the homeowner's quaint moniker for the modern-day great room—is patterned after an old barn. Wood-doweled red-oak beams draw the eye up eighteen feet to the exposed rafters.

DESPITE ITS CURRENT PICTURE-POSTCARD CONDITION, THIS LATE-EIGHTEENTH century clapboard Colonial was nothing short of a disaster in 1994 when Stewart Skolnick and Charles Haver laid claim to it. With falling plaster, wiring of fire-hazard caliber, and a heating system that was old during the Eisenhower administration, the house was a colossal project—even for an architect and an antiques dealer. Fortunately for them, however, it did have quite a distinguished beginning.

Situated in historic Roxbury, Connecticut, the late Georgian-plan house was built for Phineas Smith, the town's first state representative and a rather enterprising lawyer, which explains how it came by such fine bones and even finer aesthetics, uncommon for its rural setting. While the new owners had their work cut out for them, all original details were intact, from elaborate Adam-style moldings to exquisite tiled

Center-hall Colonial circa 1796

A RESTORATION OF CHARACTER

mantels. Even most of the oak floors were well preserved, though some twenty layers of paint had to be hand stripped from portions once concealed by rugs (a souvenir of shrewd 1950s renovation economics).

Haver and Skolnick treated their newly plastered walls with simulated whitewash—a thick paint that replicates the texture of early plaster when applied with a wallpaper brush—and finished the woodwork in period-true shades from the paint collections of Colonial Williamsburg and Stulb's Old Village. They were spared having to labor much in the kitchen. Located in an 1850s addition, it had been thoughtfully restored in the 1960s with a vintage soapstone sink and cabinets constructed from eighteenth-century doors.

The exterior, however, was a different story. Before Skolnick could begin to paint the clapboard in Williamsburg's Payton Randolph Grey, he had to remove two hundred years of colors, including the original brick red (extremely popular at that time). Yet he took some consolation from the task: It enabled him to observe firsthand the fickle history of American house fashion.

★ Despite its various makeovers—including the hipped-roof, Classical portico added in the 1820s and the one-story addition thirty years later—the façade of this late-eighteenth-century gentleman-farmer's house has aged remarkably well. Little original clapboard had to be replaced once they were stripped of layers of paint; all six-over-six-light windows, dating to about 1850, are still intact. Only the Ionic capitals on the portico's paired columns had to be reconstructed.

★ An eighteenth-century-style trestle table and Windsor chairs summon an old tavernlike spirit in the dining room (opposite), corroborated by the vintage lantern-cum-chandelier and the tin candle sconces (all electrified) that line the whitewashed walls. ★ Framed by shuttered windows, a European baroque mirror (above) bestows grandeur on the study, apropos of its front-parlor pedigree. Floating above a curvaceous Chippendale-style sofa, the 1750 jewel is hung from a picture rail, added by the owners to preserve the walls.

★ An impressive selection of English Delft tiles—quite popular in Colonial times as a decorative element (not to mention a sign of affluence)—embellish the slip on three of the house's four fireplaces. The most elaborate were reserved for the two front (read "public") parlors. The classic Adam-style mantel (opposite and above left), whose sepia-tone tiles are unusual if not rare, resides in what the owners call the study. Brass candlesticks—three French and one Spanish, all mid eighteenth century—flank a nineteenth-century American Neoclassical mirror. ★ The plain-fronted mantel (above right), painted a deep early-American blue to complement its serene-hued Bible scenes, occupies the den. One of the two original rooms at the rear of the house (the dining room, née keeping room, is the other), it was previously the birthing room, which perhaps explains the choice of tiles. ★ The stylish chip-carved mantel (right), another example of Adam fashion, holds court in the living room with the disarming tile design of whimsically painted soldiers.

★ The front hall hosts a variety of chip-carved moldings (above)—masterful examples of Federal ornamentation as interpreted in the more rural vernacular. Yet the original divided door, with its plain board lining and paneled exterior, reveals earlier, Colonial roots. ★ Continuing the hall's high style, a Georgian staircase (opposite) is punctuated with gracefully carved brackets. The inherited burgundy-painted floor was retained for its mahoganylike richness.

WITH ONLY TWO ROOMS AND THE DISPOSITION OF AN OLD MULE PLUMB OUT of kicks, the low-slung, log farmhouse in the hill country of central Texas had one saving grace: a front porch so perfectly situated, it could coax a breeze out of the stillest of Texas dog days. For interior-design consultants Larry and Karen Beevers, city dwellers looking for a backwoods retreat, the fact that it had hardly any post-nineteenth-century improvements was an almost bigger draw.

Built during the Civil War years by George Dippel, one of the tens of thousands of Germans to immigrate to the young Republic between 1845 and 1860, the story-and-a-half farmhouse is a classic piece of Texas-German frontier architecture. Initially composed of two rooms flanking an open hallway—dubbed a dogtrot house—it was fashioned of heartwood-cedar logs held in square-notched-and-pegged construction. The gabled ends were cloaked in board-and-batten siding, the front porch in the same square-hewn hori-

LONE STAR LANDMARK
Log Dogtrot circa 1863

zontal logs that faced the interior walls. Sometime within the farmhouse's first decade, the dogtrot was enclosed and a kitchen added at the back, an upgrade from the original, separate cookhouse.

The next improvement, an indoor bathroom, wouldn't come for another hundred years, not long before the Beevers bought the 35-acre farm in 1991. And their contributions, restorative and otherwise, have kept to the tradition of rugged simplicity—from scrubbing and simply waxing the long-leaf and knotty pine floors to camouflaging their newly installed insulation with tongue-and-groove boards cut to fit around the rafters. The decor of Settlement House, as they named it, follows suit, peeling paint and all. (It doesn't hurt that their town of Round Top is home to one of the country's most celebrated antiques fairs.) Whitewashed walls are the backdrop for humble pine pieces from the mid to late 1800s, punctuated with collections of all things Texana—vintage crockery, folk art, Native American serapes, cowboy hats, and enough antlers, horns, and bleached animal skulls to make it clear that this is home on the range.

★A magnificent live oak tree (opposite), at least four hundred years old and one of six on the property, casts an early-morning shadow over the Civil War–era farmhouse. It's said that Confederate soldiers stationed on the land helped the family of German settlers erect the log frame. Beyond the oak stands one of three 1860s well houses, bearing its original red paint. The snake-rail fence surrounding the front grounds came from a neighboring farm of the same era.

★ While replacing an inauthentic and rundown tin roof with period-style cedar shingles, the owners extended the back roofline to match the front (left), augmenting the 1870s kitchen extension with a bathroom and covered back porch. To protect the long-lived siding, they stained it a smoky gray—a near match to the weathered look of unfinished cedar. ★ On the generous front porch (below), a collection of antique country chairs offers the coolest seats in the house. ★ Recent additions to the down-home-Texas charm, a Brahma bull skull (opposite) found on the property keeps watch over a bronze door knocker in the shape of a longhorn— the mascot of the University of Texas, alma mater of both homeowners.

★ Relics of a colorful heritage—including a pine sofa (opposite), reupholstered in rawhide and made cozy with pillows covered in vintage serapes—outfit the living room with rich character. Deer antlers, draped with homespun swags, top the six-over-six windows, through which the hand-hewn cedar porch rafters can be seen. ★ The enclosed dogtrot (above) is a gold mine of nineteenth-century frontier-family artifacts. An electrified gas lamp hangs from the whitewashed cedar-plank ceiling.

★ Like its mirror-opposite "pen" across the dogtrot, the dining room (left) is decked with Texas farm furniture—a 9-foot-long pine table, German pie safe, dry sink—and vintage cast-iron masonry stars that appoint the windows. Dining benches were salvaged from an old, rural Texas church; the pierced-tin six-arm candle chandelier was made by a modern-day local tinsmith. ★ An antique wrought-iron bed with brass accents and a granny quilt (above) is the focal point of the master bedroom, which the homeowners carved out of a corner of the kitchen addition at the rear of the house. Flanking the oil-cloth rodeo poster are framed primitive paintings by twentieth-century Louisiana folk artist, Clementine Hunter.

CHARM WAS NEVER HIGH ON THE COLONISTS' LIST OF PRIORITIES, WHAT with food, safety, and basic shelter proving to be all-consuming concerns. Yet, however inadvertently, charm found a way to inform the character of this First Period farmhouse situated in the village of East Marion on the northern-most tip of New York's Long Island.

The diminutive, cedar-shingled dwelling has all the makings of an English country cottage—never mind that it was home to generations of potato farmers until well into the twentieth century. One of three houses built in the mid 1600s by the Salmon brothers, who are said to have come down the coast from Connecticut to settle their families, it's the only structure to have survived. Originally comprising two rooms—a hall-and-parlor plan with a sleeping loft—the story-and-a-half dwelling gained a living room, master bedroom and bath, and two upstairs guest rooms in 1939 with an addition commissioned by

SIMPLY CHARMING
**Shingled Cottage
circa 1647**

Brooklyn businessman James Kent. Still of modest scale by modern standards, the farmhouse remained in the Kent family until 1988, when Rosa Ross, a caterer and cookbook author, and her creative-director husband, Ronald, purchased it as their weekend retreat.

Except for having to upgrade the kitchen, the Manhattan couple faced mostly cosmetic work. They relieved the pine floors, built-in hutches, and three fireplace mantels of their somber paint. From Stulb's

Old Village Paints, a selection of historically accurate shades, they chose a Colonial blue for both the stair risers and shutters and Wild Bayberry for the living room woodwork. Antique Redouté botanical prints from Ross's collection grace many of the walls. Coincidentally, these depict flowers from the garden she inherited around the house—a not-so-coincidentally English cottage garden.

★ The farmhouse owes much of its English-cottage disposition to its weathered, native cedar shingles (opposite), common to early Long Island homes. Original batten shutters, in a classic Colonial hue expand on the cottage charm. ★ Towering trees close to the house (above), originally planted for protection from the elements, now also provide privacy.

★ The dining room's built-in corner cupboard (above left), an early farmhouse staple, illustrates the settlers' skill in utilizing every inch of space. Its crown molding was a much later addition. ★ The dentil molding and pilasters that ornament the mantel (above right) were probably an eighteenth-century attempt to add a bit of formality to the room; likewise the primitive carvings that embellish the pieces. ★ Although the living room (left) is part of the later addition, its design is respectful of the farmhouse's roots. The mantel, previously located in the hall, was moved to front a Rumford fireplace. The owners chose a period green for the molding and trim. ★ The pine paneling that lines one living room wall is a rustic front for the master bedroom (opposite), which includes a reproduction Shaker-style tester bed and pine side table, a flea-market find.

FOR A TIME IN AND AROUND ITHACA, NEW

York, grain was the new gold. Farmers prospered, evidenced by the many Greek Revival–style farmhouses of gleaming white clapboard that graced the landscape of the Finger Lakes region. One such house is Hitch Lyman's, which was built for an affluent farm family in the mid-1800s at the height of the area's prosperity.

Fast-forward little more than a hundred years, and this architectural gem stood empty, abandoned like so many of its neighbors—and about to be fodder for the wrecking ball. Enter Victoria Romanoff and Sarah Adams, local preservationists, whose firm not only returned the farmhouse to its original stature but

Greek Revival circa 1847

CLASSICAL GRACE

first had to move it to make way for a new highway. Two fields and a small stream later, the farmhouse was relocated to 4 pastoral acres. Graciously restored by the time Lyman, a landscape designer, bought it, all that remained to be done was a kitchen renovation. And even with that, he had a head start. Romanoff and Adams had already extended the kitchen, located in the wing, by about fifteen feet. They also removed its ceiling, thereby creating the perfect shell for a larger, modern room. Lyman took complete advantage of this extra space by building a fireplace (the two-story height offered ample room for the flue) and placing the scullery around the corner (to keep dirty dishes from view).

Except for a well-edited selection of period furnishings, Lyman has left the rest of the house deliberately unadorned and uncluttered: No window dressing to detract from the majestic surrounds of the six-over-six windows; only an occasional carpet swatch on the worn pine floors. Yet such spareness doesn't translate to stark. Here, the classical simplicity warms and welcomes all on its own.

★ This upstate New York farmhouse deftly demonstrates why Greek Revival reigned for much of the mid nineteenth century. The front-gabled, corner-pilastered façade (opposite), with its elaborate moldings—thirteen different ones from the peak down—defines the understated difference from the style's antebellum Southern interpretation. ★ In keeping with the spirit of the house's agricultural roots, its owner opted for minimal landscaping (above) and maintains a simple mown path to the front door.

★Furnishings in the double parlor (left and above) concede center stage to the elegant classical proportions. Thirteen-inch-wide door and window surrounds, made of tulip poplar, a smooth, knot-free wood, add a generous note to the space. Paneled folding doors divide the rooms and a mirror-image pair of faux fireplaces. (Since the wood-burning stove had rendered working fireplaces unnecessary, such ornamental mantelpieces were the era's antidote to blank walls.) A backdrop of warm, creamy ivory flatters the light-filled living rooms; dark wood tones add defining contrast in an antique ogee-frame mirror, poised on the front parlor's mantel, and a birdcage Windsor armchair. ★ Likewise, the shapely, black-stained newel post and balusters (right) highlight the all-white staircase.

★ The staircase's column, with its nautical-inspired cap (opposite), epitomizes the inventive spirit of the times. Probably inspired by a pattern book, the design is patently unique (read "made up"); even the "fluted" column is a clever fabrication made by joining together a dozen two-by-fours. ★ Wall-to-wall, built-in bookshelves (above) transformed the original attic into an intimate library. Charming, if threadbare, rugs from the owner's eclectic collection of "carpet ghosts" punctuate the rooms and hallways.

★ The new kitchen fireplace (opposite), raised off the floor for easier access, replicates the style of the double parlor's mantels; the graduated-step design on its camouflaged flue is reminiscent of eighteenth-century furniture. ★ The wide parlor door (above), once called the "coffin door" (for obvious reasons), leads to the back terrace, which is shaded by a trained canopy of trees. "Temple Shirley," a regal lawnmower shed designed in Greek Revival style by the owner, stands in the background.

REINVENTING

By its nature, the farmhouse is a forgiving architectural form. After all, these were houses that farmers added entire wings and stories to, grafted on whole new styles, and occasionally even picked up and moved. They were built for and with practicality, never too precious or pedigreed to be tampered with. It is this malleable quality that enabled farmhouses to stay current with prevailing tastes and modern advancements, from indoor plumbing to electricity. This also explains their architectural inconsistencies and idiosyncracies—the very characteristics that can make farmhouses so fascinating. But it's also this quirkiness that persistently trips up the purist, the architectural historian, and anyone searching for clear definitions or nomenclature.

Today, owners might not be quite so quick to physically resite their homes; nor is there a single, widespread aesthetic they would adopt in the way many Victorians imposed Carpenter Gothic details on an unsuspecting Colonial, for example. Instead, owners are reinterpreting what farmhouse style means to them. Their roots may no longer be of the land, yet the appeal of country life still draws.

They're continuing the vernacular tradition by taking a more personal approach: introducing a present-tense palette or mixing twentieth-century designs with period furnishings. They're also selectively updating by enlarging rooms and creating outdoor patios

THE FARMHOUSE

and living spaces, almost nonexistent in the original houses. While their restorations may not be literal, they are nonetheless true to the farmhouse spirit—which, by definition, allows for and even embraces reinvention.

FOR ALL ITS CALCULATED SIMPLICITY, THERE IS NOTHING PLAIN ABOUT the Quaker building tradition. Certainly not in any boring sense of the word. That's why it's hard for interior designer Laura Bohn and her husband, builder Richard Fiore, to identify what about the Bucks County, Pennsylvania, farmhouse first seduced them: its orderly lines or ramshackle state.

As professionals, they could appreciate the disciplined symmetry and efficiency of design that characterize the stone farmhouses of the area, settled by communities of English Quakers as far back as the late 1600s. Perhaps *because* they're professionals, they couldn't resist the challenge of an all-out renovation. Most likely, they found both factors equally irresistible for making this their weekend haven.

Dating from the late eighteenth century, the house was built as a single room—the hall with a fireplace the size of a small Jeep—plus a sleeping loft. An 1830s addition to the front comprised twin parlors

Story-and-a-half Cottage late 1700s

NEW RUSTIC STYLE

(one for men and one for women, each with its own entrance, suggesting the home was also used as a meetinghouse) and a full second floor with three bedrooms. This is probably also when its exterior was stuccoed, a fashionably formal look for stone farmhouses of that era. A century and a half later, Bohn and Fiore contributed a generous flagstone terrace, followed by a kitchen wing with breakfast nook, pantry, and a much needed downstairs bathroom.

They also contributed a wonderful, comfortable mood to the old farmhouse. Rooms, while refreshingly spare, exude warmth and character. Credit Bohn's careful edit of furnishings: a mix of her own contemporary designs—leather sofas, wooden tables with handsome lines and rich grains—and informal antiques. She limited her palette to neutrals and pales, enlivened with a dark, silvery celadon—a modern-day equivalent of the earthy Colonial green found on several of the older pieces scattered throughout the house. The result is a look that feels both vintage and modern, cozy and confident—perfectly suited to a farmhouse with roots in three centuries.

★ With a nod to the farmhouse's signature Pennsylvania Quaker symmetry, an old 6-foot-tall mail sorter is reinvented as a home for disparate *objets*. The kooky collection lightens the mood of an antique sepia print and a late-nineteenth-century portrait. Artfully propped against the gridlike chamber, they—like the stray collectibles—take on something of a capricious feel.

★Creating a lush, verdant landscape, centuries-old plantings—including boxwood and a pair of bride-and-groom maples, courtesy of the Quaker couple who built the two-story addition on what is now the back of the house (left)—are joined by the more recent arrival of hydrangeas and hostas. Side-by-side entrances access mirror-image sitting rooms, part of the 1830s addition and reflecting the Quaker tradition of providing men and women separate-but-equal accommodations for worship. ★Added in the 1980s, the south-facing flagstone terrace (above), with its wisteria arbor, makes for languid alfresco dining. The pair of wooden benches against the wall, no doubt originally used as pews, came with the house.

★ The paneled fireplace wall is the focal point of the dining room, the oldest portion of the farmhouse, which still bears its original pumpkin-pine floor. Featuring a walk-in fireplace, with raised-panel folding doors for closing it off in summer, the wall includes storage cupboards and a door that opens onto a narrow staircase to the former sleeping loft. To achieve an aged finish on the paneling, the homeowner stripped and bleached it, then rubbed it with a mix of thinned-out paint.

★ At the other end of the room, an eighteenth-century cupboard was the inspiration for the silvery-green color of the interior doors. The table, which the homeowner designed and treated to the same aging process as the paneling, is of rough-cut cedar. The rustic-modern wrought-iron candle chandelier gets illumination aid from halogen lights hidden among the ceiling beams. Side-by-side parlors added in the 1830s reflect a more contemporary lifestyle.

★ Tucked beneath a gable, the original sleeping quarters (above) is now a guest room. Endearing for its diminutive scale— standing upright is possible only under the ridgepole (except, that is, for Amy, the family Corgi)—the little room was a big challenge to furnish. The double bed had to be hoisted, in sections, through a window, and a lift-top Shaker chest became a fitting alternative to a bureau. Scratch-coat plaster on walls and ceiling adds a rustic quality without contributing to claustrophobia, as most solid colors might. ★ In the master bedroom (opposite), part of the 1830s addition, the homeowner devised the illusion of a four-poster bed by attaching double molding to the ceiling and suspending two sets of floor-length natural linen curtains between the channels. Adding to the visual trickery is the 29-inch-tall bed with a dust ruffle of deep, height-enhancing pleats. Furnishings were kept simple, if not exactly expected: An old child-size school chair sits in for a bedside table.

FOR A LITTLE PLACE, THE MID-NINETEENTH-CENTURY FARMHOUSE IN MOUNT

Vernon, Ohio, had a lot of style—and a lot of styles. Accenting its otherwise humble center-hall form was an abundance of architectural details, from the Greek Revival–like columned front entry and pedimented window surrounds inside to the Southern-influenced full front porch, narrow, gabled dormers, and metal roof. This vernacular overachiever, perhaps the handiwork of a frustrated architect (and owner of several pattern books), would have been something to see in its day. By the time Kevin Reiner and Chuck Ross spotted it in 1999, though, the farmhouse had been abandoned for seven years and, except to the family of raccoons living it up in the attic, no longer looked like much.

Thus began a two-year labor of love, as Reiner and Ross, both with day jobs in the horticulture trade, spent their nights and weekends repairing and renovating every rundown square inch. With true period

**Porch-façade
Greek Revival
circa 1840**

RESCUE MISSION

restoration not an option—in the 1930s, a nearby house of similar scale and vintage but devoid of any ornamentation had been fitted onto the back—the two chose to be faithful to the farmhouse's humble, if ambitious, spirit. They also chose to be pragmatic: replacing crumbled plaster with longer-lasting drywall, for instance; equipping the front porch with a ceiling of new beadboard and a floor of new tongue-and-groove planks; adding a second bathroom. Colorwise, they took a fresh approach, using a palette of sophis-

ticated pastels to transcend the interior's split-personality architecture.

Barely a year after the paint dried, Reiner and Ross sold their little masterpiece to Sue Reiss, a retail executive so taken with its charms that she didn't change a thing. Her furnishings, a mix of sweet antiques and later Americana, are a perfect match to the contemporary-country mood. Now the little farmhouse is once again big on style.

★Topping the central-Ohio farmhouse (opposite) is a mostly original sheet-metal roof, recently painted artichoke green. The bay window is an example of how houses were updated in the late 1800s. ★A cast-iron foot from an old tub (left), which the homeowner refinished in a vibrant blue, serves as a doorstop for the master bath.

★ The dining room (left and right), in the back addition, achieves dressed-down elegance from a careful pairing of unmatched elements. The centerpiece is a new take on the farmhouse table, made from salvaged planks and a whitewashed base, surrounded by a set of 1920s Louis XVI-style chairs that once sat in the famed Waldorf-Astoria Hotel. The crystal chandelier, of similar vintage, lends a romantic quality. Adorning the mint-green walls are imitation ironstone plates, artfully hung with ribbons; a series of lithographs of Morris bird eggs, circa 1879, and vintage botanical prints of pears from a Paris flea market. ★ On the opposite wall (right), a music cabinet, circa 1900, finds new purpose, housing linens and showcasing a collection of Depression glass celery vases. Above it, an elaborately carved picture frame is a work of art all by itself. Between the pair of windows, a 1920s enamel-top writing-table-turned-sideboard displays a trio of old cranberry glass cake plates.

★ A dramatically styled hexagonal table from the early twentieth century takes center stage in the living room's bay window (above). ★ Pieces from the home-owner's collection of pressed-glass compotes (above left) create a glistening still life. Across from the sofa, 1820s Sheraton-style armchairs (below left) add a sense of history to the conversation area. ★ The walls and floor of a guest room (opposite) in the front of the house were painted in watery shades of blue for a floating effect. The antique quilt on the bed augments the soothing appeal. A casement window, original to the dormer, helps to fill the room with sunlight.

THE 1960S WERE THE BEST OF TIMES AND THE WORST OF TIMES FOR THIS

Greek Revival farmhouse. The decade's style arbiters had deemed antiques a thing of the past, preferring new materials and modern looks. Clearly, this mid-nineteenth-century farmhouse was desperate for an update—which explains how its stately white clapboard came to be covered with vinyl siding, its wood floors with shag carpeting, and its walls and trim with a combination of flocked paper and barn siding. It wasn't for another three decades, when new owners Michel and Patricia Jean began restoring their Dutchess County, New York, home, that the true beauty of such misguided alterations would be revealed.

The various forms of camouflage had served, however inadvertently, as protective coating. Once they were removed, wonderfully well-preserved original surfaces were discovered. Not that the farmhouse didn't still need considerable work. The residence of a successful dairy farmer and his family in its heyday,

A COLORFUL PAST

Greek Revival circa 1845

the place had been converted into a two-family house in (when else?) the 1960s. As a result, the Jeans had plenty of dismantling to do before they could even attempt their wish-list renovation.

For these owners of a French restaurant in Manhattan's SoHo district, a hard-working kitchen was de rigueur. They turned an 1890 kitchen–pantry–utility-closet addition into one spacious room, building in a fireplace with a wood-burning oven and adding on a terrace. Equally important was restoration of the farmhouse's original proportions: They deferred to the Greek Revival detailing and scale—dramatic window and door surrounds and 10-foot-high ceilings. Their signature imprint? Wonderfully colored walls—a mix of warm pastels and bold, hot brights—which make for a most pleasant surprise in an otherwise respectfully white house.

★ Reconstructed from an old photo, the cozy portico (opposite) honors its Neoclassical predecessor with Doric columns, pilaster trim, and sidelights framing the door. Louvered shutters, mostly repaired originals, warm the white façade. ★ A less common, if no less grand, variation on the front-gabled motif, the Greek Revival farmhouse (right) is distinguished by corner pilasters and pedimented gable ends.

★ Living-room walls glazed in warm persimmon over yellow are the perfect foil for the fanciful window surrounds (left and opposite). Though the room is furnished with an eye to the past—from the American Empire mantel mirror to the Shaker-style blanket chest serving as a coffee table—the blue-accented palette keeps it from feeling old-fashioned. ★ Several early-twentieth-century fruit illustrations, whose juicy colors complement the room, frame an eighteenth-century desk (below). ★ Neoclassical moldings form the window surround (opposite), crowned, like most others in the house, with a dentil-decorated pediment. The tin mirror-backed sconce is one of a pair flanking the fireplace.

★ With its marble-top beadboard island, glass-fronted cabinetry, and space-saving wrought-iron pot rack, the renovated kitchen (left) blends the farmhouse's nineteenth-century feel with the restaurateur-homeowners' twenty-first-century needs. Installing a west-facing wall of multipaned casement windows opened the room to sweeping views of the Catskills. On the floor, Pennsylvania bluestone shimmers in the light. ★ A modern pendant fixture (top right) works wonderfully over the vintage-style French farmhouse table, partnered with a set of early Connecticut spindle-back chairs. ★ Tucked into a corner nook, an old pine cupboard (bottom right) showcases majolica plates and vintage enameled canisters from France. The period-influenced cabinetry is finished with an ocher wash for a look that spans the centuries.

★Dressed in a riot of outspoken hats, a Victorian faux-bamboo hat stand (opposite) greets visitors upon arrival. Dark-red walls animate the library, once the front parlor, where less ornamented window surrounds bear a flame-mahogany finish. The staircase's heavy, turned newel post is classic Greek Revival. ★The spacious second-floor landing (above) enjoys the mixed company of several centuries of furnishings: a graceful Victorian hallway settee, designed for removing boots upon entering a home; an old French rope basket (which the owners call the "snake charmer's basket"); and, anchoring the back wall, a pair of early-American slat-back chairs. Overhead, an electrified antique Chinese lantern adds to the eclectic flavor, casting a glow on the butter-hued walls.

BESIDES TWO LIVING-ROOM BAY WINDOWS AND WHAT REMAINED OF THE WELL-endowed interior moldings, the rectangular box of a house in Winnetka, Illinois, had little to recommend it—at least on the surface. Its less obvious assets—good bones and a Victorian-farmhouse heritage—were enough to capture the imagination of architect Paul Konstant when he signed on to expand and build character back into the once noble homestead.

Winnetka, settled in the first half of the 1800s predominantly by German immigrants and second- and third-generation New Englanders lured by generous land grants, was perfectly situated for commercial-crop farming. Being just eighteen miles north of Chicago, a stone's throw from the Green Bay Trail post road, and by 1854 a stop on the Chicago & Milwaukee Railroad line, the village prospered. Consequently, it was graced with handsome farmhouses in Greek or Gothic Revival style, which later often acquired

Gable-front Victorian circa 1856

ALL ABOUT NOSTALGIA

Italianate accents. Konstant referred to these architectural influences when he designed the renovation.

The extension—a side-gabled wing, added at a right angle to the existing structure—comprises kitchen, dining room, family room, and mudroom (a necessary concession to contemporary family life), with the master suite and another bedroom and bath above, all in keeping with the scale of the original house. Likewise, the interior decoration channels the spirit of the typical nineteenth-century American farmhouse. For most rooms, designers Lee Bierly and Christopher Drake chose a pale palette trimmed in creamy-white molding, reproduced to match the house's original casings. (True to the period, even the baseboards are striking: crowned and nine inches high.) Furnishings are a well-selected combination of vintage reproductions and interpretations and country antiques. Even the living room's bay windows, a distinctive Italianate feature, are dressed in silk-taffeta panels as opposed to heavy, formal draperies—as with everything else, reflecting the simple, yet stylish, farmhouse rendition of American Victorian.

★ The remodeled farmhouse's two-story gable-front-and-wing design, also called an L-house, was popular in the rural Midwest and Northeast in the mid to late 1800s. Complementing the period style of the original bay windows, the exterior sports other Italianate-influenced elements: the door canopy with a modified arch, two-over-two sash windows, and—perhaps the most nostalgic feature—a gracious, three-sided wraparound porch, appointed with charming hand-turned columns and balusters.

★ Part of the new addition, the butler's pantry (opposite) at the east end of the kitchen is patterned after the Victorian house staple. Glass-fronted cabinets, soapstone countertops, and V-groove paneling (standing in for the classic beadboard) combine for timeless appeal. The antique eel rakes add a graphic quality to the all-white room. ★ A lanternlike chandelier and the wavy, ribbed splats of the Chippendale-inspired chairs (right) throw the dining room a few curves. Buttery-yellow wallpaper forms a fresh backdrop for the grid of Matisse linocuts. ★ In the remodeled original living room (below left and right), ebony-hued furnishings and accent pieces (basaltware teapots, circular mirror) provide a painterly contrast to linen-covered walls. Lending an illusion of height, the bay window's unstructured fabric panels attach at the ceiling, draping to the floor.

★ Derivative of sack-back Windsor chairs, a settee (left) sits against a wall outside the mudroom with pieces of an old model biplane echoing its lines. ★ A fresh take on the French classic, toile de Jouy dresses three walls and the dust ruffle in the master bedroom (below). Against the pattern, the high-post bed, dating to the early 1800s, and a pedestal card table of slightly later vintage strike engaging silhouettes. Matching sets of French nineteenth-century men's dressing-area dishes find new purpose as wall art.

HAVING BEEN RENOVATED IN ITS EARLY YEARS, AS MOST NEW ENGLAND farmhouses were—on a need-to-grow basis—this diminutive Colonial took on some rather curious proportions. It was this eccentric quality that instantly appealed to Jeff McKay when he was looking for a weekend house some fifteen years ago. With multiple generations' worth of possessions growing ever older in storage, the advertising maven needed a place in which his hodgepodge of family heirlooms could comfortably coexist. Where better than a quirky late-eighteenth-century farmhouse with a pair of second-story windows at floor level and a master bedroom barely big enough for a bed?

There's even a similarly organic quality to the way McKay furnished the farmhouse. Though his ancestral accumulation had supplied him with such treasures as an American Empire mahogany daybed, assorted hand-embroidered quilts, and more than a few trophy animal heads, he was light on the basics—

**Eyebrow Colonial
circa 1780**

FLIGHT OF FANCY

a real bed and a dining table, for instance. With no preconceived design scheme and the budget of a new homeowner, McKay began scouring thrift shops and flea markets for all the necessities of home. His forays over those first few years netted the kind of stash to do his pack-rat background proud; and his inimitable aesthetic, honed by an art school background and years of running his own ad agency, made everything work together in wonderfully irreverent fashion.

In addition to furnishings from some of the best and worst design periods of the twentieth century—including a few homespun pieces that defy classification, to say nothing of logic—there are several dozen framed paintings to match. These McKay displays in a little room added to the back of the house, along with a new kitchen, in the 1970s. Appropriately named the "gallery room," it is floor to ceiling artwork—just one of the current owner's many witty expressions in a house built by the wits of its earlier owners.

★ The landing was once the farmhouse's dormitory-style sleeping loft, which accounts for its ample dimensions. Remedying the lack of upstairs storage space, the homeowner recently built in a wall-to-wall cabinet. Made from salvaged barn siding and fronted with carpenter's-cloth mesh, it was whitewashed like the rest of the landing. A mid-century-modern chair partnered with a late-Victorian bible stand exemplifies the house's eclectic collaborations. On the thrift-shop bureau, a recent Eva Zeisel vase echoes the milky white of the opaque glassware from the 1950s.

★ From the front (left), the "eyebrow Colonial"—so called for the two tiny windows centered just below the eaves—still reflects its proud Connecticut-Yankee heritage. Those bottom-hinged windows, an early attempt to gain light without losing heat, hit floor level in the master bedroom, making for interesting illumination.
★ Inspired by its wooded surroundings, the house is painted dark brown with leaf-green trim (above). The sole departure is the coral of the original batten door—a touch of the unexpected, in keeping with what resides within.

★ The dining room (left) is uniquely outfitted with a nineteenth-century harvest refectory table and set of 1920s birch-twig chairs from Maine. The two crudely constructed end chairs and matching console table, tag-sale acquisitions, are among the owner's favorite handcrafted oddities. The cast-iron antler candlesticks come from his tiny hometown in Indiana; the branch and bird's nest floating near the ceiling beam from his own backyard. ★ The collection of 1930s Desert Sand pottery from California (above) was inherited from the homeowner's father. ★ His grandmother's splendid American Empire daybed (opposite) is all but upstaged by a slew of questionable-quality paintings. To make peace with the terra-cotta-tiled floor, here and in the dining room, the homeowner hand painted a checkerboard border using whitewash and dark-green deck paint.

★ The south living room (left) has 12- and 15-foot-long floor-boards, suggesting that the original owner was fairly well off. Seasonal muslin slipcovers unify the mix of family pieces and thrift-shop finds. In winter, the furnishings feature velvet upholstery in differing jewel tones for each cushion, pillow, and frame. ★ Not one to miss an opportunity for whimsy, the homeowner uses a tiny cabinet that started life as a dresser drawer (above), to showcase his set of 1950s turquoise opaque water goblets in the dining room.

IF MOST OLD HOUSES TELL A STORY OF ONE OR TWO DESIGN PERIODS, THIS

Cross River, New York, farmhouse reads more like an architectural anthology. Built at the end of the 1700s in refined Adam style—a three-story box with a slightly pitched hipped roof—the house acquired a host of architectural embellishments over the next hundred years. A front porch with slim columns and pilasters flanking both the entry and twin casement doors demonstrates the transition to Greek Revival; its cast-iron railings display late-Neoclassical motifs. The paneled frieze and eaves brackets, suggestive of an Italianate influence, were likely appointed when the east wing was added, around the turn of the twentieth century.

Such a mix of elements could have confounded most modern-day restorers, who often pursue loyalty to a particular vintage. But this disparity is what attracted Heidi and David Johnston when they purchased the property some six years ago. It was inconceivable for the Johnstons (she the owner of The Yellow

Adam-style Colonial circa 1798

ECLECTIC REVIVAL

Monkey, a nearby antiques shop, he a bond trader by day and antiques delivery guy by night) to strip the façade of any ornamentation. Their only reasonable choice, then, recommended by their restoration architect, Joel Trace, would be to renovate—respectfully—in the same eclectic vein.

To that end, the front casement doors and their interior surrounds were replicated, with one set installed in the dining room to balance the facade and another at the opposite end of the living room, opening onto the enlarged kitchen-family room. New kitchen windows were fabricated in the farmhouse's classic Greek Revival six-over-six style. The roof on the addition was raised to meet the original roofline—with the oddly low ceiling of the dining room gaining height as a result—and as a subtle unifying element, the same style frieze and eaves brackets were carried all the way around.

Decorating was less of a dilemma, considering the couple's access to nineteenth-century European country antiques (the shop's specialty), as well as Heidi Johnston's fabric- and furniture-design background. Fittingly, the decor rivals the exterior in period eclecticism, creating comfort that is naturally timeless.

★ With high-ceilinged rooms above a raised basement, the New York farmhouse is reminiscent of many eighteenth-century Colonials in the Deep South. Cast-iron porch railings, added in the mid to late 1800s, contribute to the Southern flavor of the house; their predecessors were most likely wooden and a continuation of the stairway's square balusters.

★ Illustrative of the house's aesthetic evolution, the living room (right) was reconfigured, probably in the early 1900s, from the original double parlor. Two intimate conversation areas, linked by a pair of Art Deco armchairs and two Louis XV–style *fauteuils*, visually cut the 20-foot-long room down to size. A Biedermeier secretary showcases a landscape of 1940s Floraline vases. ★ Both the *fauteuil* and sofa (above) sport fabrics designed by the homeowner for the celebrated fabrics house Scalamandré.

★ Reflecting a taste for the eclectic, a crystal chandelier (opposite) in fancy French Empire style keeps company with a Swedish country tallcase clock that still wears its original nineteenth-century paint. A set of modern-looking, cotton-duck-upholstered Parsons chairs, from The Yellow Monkey Furniture private label, complements a reproduction nineteenth-century birdcage-pedestal table handcrafted of yew. Having expanded the dining room by sixteen feet, the architect was able to retain the light-filled room's hundred-year-old windows, although casings and base moldings had to be replicated. ★ One of a pair of painted Chinese Chippendale-style occasional tables (above) is awarded an array of trophy cups, antiques-fair finds. ★ The homeowner designed this built-in buffet shelving unit (top right) as much to conceal the dining room's massive radiator as to display her collection of blue-and-white transferware. ★ Between a pair of new exterior casement doors, made to match those on the front porch, a handmade family heirloom (right) is home to a sparkly collection of mercury glass.

LIVING IN AN OLD HOUSE CAN SOMETIMES MAKE ONE BELIEVE IN GHOSTS. How else to explain a slipper falling from a closet ceiling, the mysterious repair of a sugar bowl, objects disappearing and reappearing in odd places—all "natural" occurrences within the first months of the new owner's arrival at this cottage-size, eighteenth-century farmhouse. After one too many bouts of things going bump in the night, the homeowner made an announcement: She promised to take good care of the ramshackle old place, if they would only knock it off. And with that, a peaceful coexistence ensued.

As spirits go, these were certainly pedigreed—from Moore Gibbs, one of the first settlers of Litchfield County, Connecticut, and a soldier in the Revolutionary War, for whom the house was built in the late 1700s; to Sarah Francis Walkey, the last, and much loved, Congregational church pastor to live there, a hundred fifty years later. The current resident, a design director at a Manhattan art museum who bought the house

COUNTRY ARTISTRY

Cape Cod circa 1786

in 1999, was certainly true to her word. From putting on a new shingled roof to lifting layers of decrepit linoleum off the kitchen floor, she gave the farmhouse back its unassuming dignity.

She deftly refreshed the interior with gallons of white paint, completely camouflaging the fact that the house is small and dark (though hardly unhandsome). White walls with high-gloss white trim create a luminous canvas for her trove of whimsical treasures—many themselves white and most acquired long before she owned a country house, a small one no less. The mix is nothing if not picturesque, and while few pieces were chosen for their provenance, each has a tale to tell—the sum total of which speaks volumes on the subject of rustic elegance. Not bad for a haunted house.

★ Arranged with artistic sleight of hand, old and new pieces comfortably cohabit (opposite): modern artisanal chairs join a vintage butcher's table; newly installed beadboard adds Colonial character; a primitive seed cupboard has been promoted to pantry duty.
★ The original flat-paneled front door (above), painted cranberry red, is a style more typical of interior doors. The shallow hood and five-light transom, however, were common to farmhouses of this era—smartly accenting the entry without the cost of a porch.

★Lending something of an ethereal air, a white ironstone plate and pair of cast-porcelain heads (top left) occupy a corner cupboard in the living room. In one of the home's rare minimalist appointments, a wooden planter with its shock of bright green grass is the cupboard's only other occupant. The built-in is probably a nineteenth-century modification, along with the room's paneled dado, now employed as a picture ledge. A nod to the homeowner's love of French style, an antique Louis XV–style settee was fittingly reupholstered in toile de Jouy. ★Bounded by a gleaming ash floor, the living room (bottom left) is a study in cozy chic, dressed serenely in a dozen shades—all of them white. Color is welcomed in small moments: The homeowner's signature pink roses in an antique silver pitcher, a vintage grape-cluster lamp in tan marble, and the ochre toile pillow seem to further illuminate the pale. ★In a painterly display of tone on tone, a wealth of humble white ironstone (opposite) lines the built-in cabinet. Probably added in the 1850s when the farmhouse became a parsonage, it has shallow shelves suggesting it was used for prayer-book storage. A tiny closet to the right still has its original wrought-iron heart-design handle.

★ Straddling centuries-old and contemporary styles, the homeowner chose a dramatic pewter green to envelop the study (above) and designed the carved-wood Neo-Georgian-meets-SoHo mantelpiece as its focal point. Unable to find window treatments to complement the singular palette, she made her own—painting stripes with the wall color on a swath of canvas and rigging Roman shades, visible in the distressed mirror. A pair of tin mirror-backed candle sconces from a Paris flea market illuminate a shelf of treasured antiques-shopping souvenirs. ★ A painting of the celebrated nineteenth-century statesman Daniel Webster presides over the front-hall desk set (opposite): a late-eighteenth-century side table and small rod-back Windsor chair of similar vintage. In an effort to make the steep stairs an easier climb for Roz, her Jack Russell terrier, the homeowner installed a canvas runner that she decoratively painted. It didn't help, but it added great charm to the plain square-baluster staircase. A series of oval tintype portraits, circa 1870, further animate the landing.

★ Continuing the white-house theme upstairs, the bath (opposite) is restored in early-twentieth-century-inspired style with a mosaic-tile floor in period chicken-wire design, beadboard on the walls and tub surround, a skirted-pedestal sink, and glass-shaded light fixtures. ★ In the master bedroom (above), the original of the three bedrooms, the sloping ceiling provides a built-in headboard. Night stands—a Gustavian Swedish table on the left and a contemporary tea table on the right, of disparate vintages but similar curves—soften the room's many angles. Layers of antique and Italian bed linens and a sybaritic supply of down-filled shams impart dreamy comfort.

LIKE SO MANY OLD FARMHOUSES, THIS TWO-STORY CLAPBOARD EXAMPLE in Southern New England evolved with the fortunes and tastes of the families who lived there. Built in the early nineteenth century in the era's popular Federal style, the center-chimney farmhouse acquired a succession of period details over the years—including Greek Revival, Italianate, and by century's end a Victorian-style front porch, complete with fancy fretwork. By the time its current owners took possession, nearly a hundred years later, it had even lost its distinctive central chimney. In fact, the abandoned farmhouse's most notable feature was its state of disrepair.

For its new owners, however, an editor and a graphic designer, the mix of styles perfectly matched their eclectic leanings. And despite the rotting floors, falling ceilings, and a wing that previously had been occupied by a small herd of goats, the house still boasted well-proportioned rooms and more than a few

Center-chimney Federal circa 1809

A LIGHT TOUCH

well-preserved details—enough to add character without imposing a particular style. Four floor-to-ceiling casement windows on the façade, no doubt Greek Revival modifications, spoke to the owners' wish for light-filled rooms, which they augmented by installing three sets of French doors along the back of the house. To enhance the play of natural light, they stained the entire ground floor white (an antidote to the patchwork of old and new wood floors, as well).

Decoratively, a quirky point/counterpoint approach satisfies the owners' love of modernism while remaining in touch with a farmhouse sensibility. While spare in concept, the house is big on personality—an engaging example of the juxtaposition of tradition and novelty.

★ With the same understated wit that warms the rest of the farmhouse, an old two-tone beadboard cupboard and kitschy plaster bust (opposite) keep company in a corner of the dining room with a pair of refined French chairs from the 1940s, a circa 1956 Saarinen table, and framed prints of eighteenth-century calligraphy. ★ In keeping with the restrained façade (above), the homeowners replaced a dilapidated Victorian porch with a more streamlined version.

★ Removing the walls between a series of tiny rooms in the smaller wing of the house netted space for a contemporary-size kitchen, never mind the resulting challenge of working around exterior walls broken up by so many windows and doors. In an equal-opportunity triumph of adaptive reuse, the owners transformed a modern industrial stainless-steel table into a hard-working island, and an old glass-fronted apothecary cabinet into a china closet. Celadon-gray walls take the modern edge off stainless-steel cabinetry and appliances, over which a George Nelson sunburst clock appears to float.

★ A set of reproduction Jacobsen chairs, paired with a late-nineteenth-century oak library table, brings a playful shock of color to the kitchen. Above, framed black-and-white photographs by Bernd and Hilla Becher, portraits of water towers in mid-twentieth-century Europe, are variations on the sculptural shapes of the furnishings. To the left, a pair of newly added French doors ushers in morning light and opens onto a bluestone patio. In the opposite corner, the worn finish of an old cupboard lends a bit of patina to the otherwise clean-lined space.

★ The homeowners went for a touch of drama by enveloping the living room (opposite) in a steely gray that echoes the marble slip of the fireplace and painting the millwork a high-gloss white for a pronounced architectural feel. In deference to the farmhouse's humble nature, mismatched sofas wear slipcovers of heavy-canvas drop-cloths; an unassuming, if funky, lucite coffee table is a knock-off of 1970s style. On the mantel, a shapely collection of Floraline vases, all flea-market finds, makes for a whimsical focal point. ★ Propped against one living room wall, a 1940s French mirror (top left) engages an Art Deco-era Giacometti floor lamp and a 1950s side chair in its original vinyl. ★ The arched doorways (bottom left) that flank the entryhall and lead into the living and dining rooms, were added a century ago to showcase the gracious pocket doors.

★ The curvaceous spiral staircase (opposite) features faceted-shaft balusters, a style popular in the latter decades of the nineteenth century. Its predecessor was probably the more humble center-hall Colonial box staircase. ★ A bedroom closet was sacrificed to expand the master bath (above), done in vintage fashion with a pedestal sink and floor tiles in the classic chicken-wire design. For a twist of the modern, the homeowners installed a luxuriously-proportioned shower stall, surrounded in glass block.

BRINGING
COUNTRY HOME

★ "Gauguin" hand-knitted and hand-braided rug, from the American Home Collection by Judi Boisson.

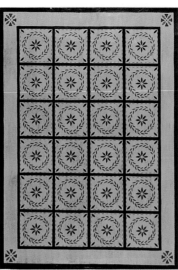

★ "Wreath" floorcloth, from Early American Floorcloths.

★ "Richmond" louver shutters with plate-mount shutter-dogs, from Vixen Hill.

ARCHITECTURAL ELEMENTS AND HARDWARE

American Heritage Shutters, Inc.
6655 Poplar Street, Suite 204
Germantown, TN 38138
(901) 751-1000
www.americanheritage
    shutters.com

Traditionally styled interior and exterior shutters

Antique Cabins and Barns
Covington, WV
(888) 941-9553
www.antiquecabinsand
    barns.com

Dismantled and reassembled hand-hewn log cabins and timber-frame barns, barn siding, antique lumber, and various vintage building materials

Antique Woods and Colonial Restorations
1273 Reading Avenue
Boyertown, PA 19512
(888) 261-4284
(610) 367-6911

Antique barns and salvaged woods

Architectural Salvage, Inc.
3 Mill Street
Exeter, NH 03833
(603) 773-5636
www.oldhousesalvage.com

Salvaged lighting and bath fixtures, hardware, mantels, doors, windows, flooring, doorknobs, stair parts, and ironwork

Architectural Salvage Warehouse
53 Main Street
Burlington, VT 05401
(892) 658-5011
www.greatsalvage.com

Salvaged architectural antiques and fixtures including mantels, doors, windows, hardware, plumbing, lighting, porch columns, and posts

Baldwin Brass
PO Box 15048
Reading, PA 19612
(800) 566-1986
www.baldwinbrass.com

Reproduction brass hardware

Ball and Ball Hardware Reproductions
463 West Lincoln Highway
(Route 30)
Exton, PA 19341
(800) 257-3711
www.ballandball.com

Reproduction hardware

Blue Ox Millworks
One X Street
Eureka, CA 95501
(800) 248-4259
www.blueoxmill.com

Historically accurate millwork, doors, and wood gutters

★ "Great Barrington," "Appleton," "White River Junction," and two "Ticking Stripes" rugs, from Woodard Weave.

★ Distressed-tin wall sconce, from Lt. Moses Willard, Inc.

★ Samples of pumpkin, marigold yellow, federal blue, bayberry green, and lexington green milk-paints, from The Old Fashioned Milk Paint Company, Inc.

Brandywine Valley Forge
PO Box 1129
Valley Forge, PA 19482
(610) 948-5116
www.bvforge.com
Hand-forged shutter, gate, and barn hardware

Crawford's Old House Store
W 1508 Marsh Road
Palmyra, WI 53156
(800) 556-7878
Corner beads and guards and wooden door stops

Cumberland Woodcraft Co.
PO Drawer 609
Carlisle, PA 17013
(800) 367-1884
www.cumberlandwood
craft.com
Wall coverings and wood corbels, brackets, moldings, paneling, lattice, cabinetry, and porch parts

Heartland Appliances, Inc.
1050 Fountain Street
Cambridge, ON N3H 4R7
Canada
(800) 361-1517
www.heartlandapp.com
Wood-burning stoves

Horton Brasses, Inc.
Nooks Hill Road
PO Box 95
Cornwall, CT 06416
(800) 754-9127
www.hortonbrass.com
Reproduction furniture and hardware in iron, brass, and hardwoods

J. S. Benson Woodworking & Design
1818 Birge Street
Brattleboro, VT 05301
(800) 339-3515
Custom-designed and histori-cally accurate doors, windows, and accessories; custom door and window hardware

Kestrel Shutters
Kestrel Manufacturing Co.
9 East Race Street
Stowe, PA 19464
(800) 494-4321
www.diyshutters.com
Raised-face, flat-panel, and louver cedar shutters

Lehman's
One Lehman Circle
PO Box 41
Kidron, OH 44636
(877) 437-5346
www.lehmans.com
Wooden barrels, grain mills, woodstoves, oil lamps, blacksmith tools, plus a wide selection of non-electric products.

Liz's Antique Hardware
435 S. LaBrea
Los Angeles, CA 90036
(323) 939-4403
www.lahardware.com
Salvaged and reproduction hardware for doors, windows, and lighting

★ "Wayside Inn, Sudsbury, MA" stencil, from MB Historic Décor.

★ "Philadelphia" board-and-batten shutters, from Timberlane Woodcrafters, Inc.

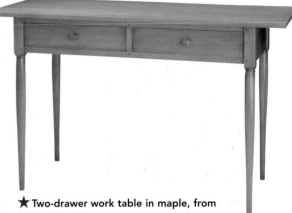

★ Two-drawer work table in maple, from Shaker Workshops.

Mantels of Yesteryear, Inc.
70 West Tennessee Avenue
McCaysville, GA 30555
(706) 492-5534
www.mantelsofyesteryear.com
Antique and reproduction mantels

Martin Senour Paints
101 Prospect Avenue
600 Guild Hall
Cleveland, OH 44115
(800) 542-8468
www.martinsenour.com
Interior and exterior paints, including the Williamsburg historic collection

MB Historic Décor
PO Box 1255
Quechee, VT 05059
(888) 649-1790
www.mbhistoricdecor.com
Historically accurate New England–style wall and floor stencils

Monroe Coldren & Son
723 E. Virginia Avenue
West Chester, PA 19380
(610) 692-5651
Reproduction American seventeenth- and eighteenth-century hardware

Ohmega Salvage
2407 San Pablo Avenue
Berkeley, CA 94703
(510) 843-7368
www.ohmegasalvage.com
Architectural details, including antique plumbing fixtures, hardware, doors, and windows

The Old Fashioned Milk Paint Company, Inc.
436 Main Street
Groton, MA 01450
(978) 448-6336
www.milkpaint.com
Genuine milk paint in a variety of colors

The Old House Parts Company
24 Blue Wave Mall
Kennebunk, ME 04043
(207) 985-1999
www.oldhouseparts.com
Architectural antiques and reproduction farmhouse furniture made from reclaimed lumber

Old Village Paint, Ltd.
PO Box 1030
Fort Washington, PA 19034
(610) 238-9001
www.old-village.com
Interior and exterior paints, including Stulb's Buttermilk Paint line of historically based colors

Restorations
1488 York Road
Carlisle, PA 17013
(717) 249-3624
www.eddonaldson.com
Restored antique hardware including doorknobs, doorbells, knockers, locks, and hinges

Shuttercraft
282 Stepstone Hill
Guilford, CT 06437
(203) 453-1973
www.shuttercraftinc.com
Traditionally styled cedar shutters

★ Pine and maple trestle table, from Shaker Workshops.

★ "Nelson-Galt" Williamsburg reproduction fence and gate, from Walpole Woodworkers.

★ "Pineapple Log Cabin" cover-up in royal blue and white, from the American Home Collection by Judi Boisson.

The Shutter Depot
437 La Grange Street
Greenville, GA 30222
(706) 672-1214
www.shutterdepot.com

Exterior and interior louver, flat-panel, and raised-panel shutters

Timberlane Woodcrafters, Inc.
197 Wissahickon Avenue
North Wales, PA 19454
(800) 250-2221
www.timberlane-wood.com

Panel, louver, and board-and-batten wooden shutters

Tremont Nail Co.
8 Elm Street
Wareham, MA 02571
(800) 842-0560
www.tremontnail.com

Historically accurate cut nails and hardware

United House Wrecking
535 Hope Street
Stamford, CT 06906
(203) 348-5371
www.unitedhouse
    wrecking.com

Architectural antiques, including stained glass, doors, windows, mantels, ironwork, and lighting and plumbing fixtures

Valspar Paint
1191 Wheeling Road
Wheeling, IL 60090
(800) 845-9061
www.valspar.com

Historically based line of interior and exterior paints

Vermont Castings
410 Admiral Boulevard
Mississauga, ON L5T 2N6
Canada
(800) 227-8683
www.vermontcastings.com

Wood-burning stoves

Vermont Soapstone Co.
248 Stoughton Pond Road
PO Box 268
Perkinsville, VT 05151
(802) 263-5404
www.vermontsoapstone.com

Soapstone sinks, countertops, and fireplaces

Vintage Barns, Wood, and Restoration, Inc.
333 Mossy Brook Road
High Falls, NY 12440
(845) 340-9870
www.vintagewoods.com

Salvaged wood, architectural details, and furniture made of reclaimed wood

Vixen Hill
Main Street
Elverson, PA 19520
(800) 423-2766
www.vixenhill.com

Fine historical shutters, panels, porch parts, and millwork

Walpole Woodworkers
767 East Street
Walpole, MA 02081
(800) 343-6948

Rustic outdoor furniture and fences, including Williamsburg reproduction fences

★ "Checkerboard Stripe" rugs, from Woodard Weave.

★ Copper and brass "Rooster" weather vane, from Good Directions.

★ "Queen Anne Slippered-Foot" table, from Bryce M. Ritter & Son.

★ One-drawer pie-safe in barn red, from Joseph Spinale Painted Furniture.

★ The "Abe Lincoln Bed," from Bryce M. Ritter & Son.

★ Cedar "Merrimack" fence and gate, from Walpole
Woodworkers.

★ Handmade reed laundry basket, from Shaker
Workshops.

★ Two-drawer, lift-top blanket chest,
from Bryce M. Ritter & Son.

★ "Little Red Schoolhouse" rug, from
Classic Rug Collection.

★ "Cambridge" chandelier, from HomArt.

★ Cornflower blue "Feathered Star" quilt, from the American Home Collection by Judi Boisson.

★ Cherry four-poster platform bed, from Thos. Moser Cabinetmakers.

★ "Benjamin Waller" Williamsburg reproduction fence and gate, from Walpole Woodworkers.

FURNITURE AND ACCESSORIES

American Period Lighting
3004 Columbia Avenue
Lancaster, PA 17603
(717) 392-5649
www.americanperiod.com
Reproductions of eighteenth-century indoor and outdoor lighting

Authentic Designs
69 Mill Road
West Rupert, VT 05776
(800) 844-9416
www.authentic-designs.com
Reproduction Early American and Colonial lighting fixtures

American Home Collection by Judi Boisson
134 Mariner Drive
Southampton, NY 11968
(631) 283-5466
www.judiboisson.com
Hand-stitched quilts and handmade rugs inspired by traditional designs

Black Ash Baskets
5066 Mott Evans Road
Trumansburg, NY 14886
(607) 387-5718
Handwoven splint baskets made from black ash

Brahms/Mount Textiles, Inc.
19 Central Street
Hallowell, ME 04347
(800) 545-9347
www.brahmsmount.com
Cotton and linen blankets manufactured on antique shuttle looms

Bryce M. Ritter & Son
100 Milford Road
Downington, PA 19335
(610) 458-0460
www.bryceritter.com
Handcrafted eighteenth- and nineteenth-century-style furniture

Chilton Shaker Collection
184 Lower Main Street
Freeport, ME 04032
(888) 510-6300
www.chiltons.com
Handcrafted Shaker-inspired furniture

Classic Rug Collection
417 16th Street
Brooklyn, NY 11215
(888) 334-0063
www.classicrug.com
Wool rugs in traditional quilt patterns

★ Cedar "Morgan" fence, from Walpole Woodworkers.

★ Sideboard table in bayberry green, from Joseph Spinale Painted Furniture.

Clay City Pottery
510 E. 14th Street
PO Box 79
Clay City, IN 47841
(800) 776-2596
www.claycitypottery.com
Hand-molded reproduction spongeware, greenware, and white stoneware

The Country Iron Foundry
65 Twelfth Street South
Naples, FL 34102
(800) 233-9945
www.firebacks.com
Traditional cast-iron firebacks

Country Road Associates, Ltd.
63 Front Street
PO Box 885
Millbrook, NY 12545
(845) 677-6041
www.countryroad associates.com
Handcrafted nineteenth-century-style furniture made from salvaged barn wood

Early American Floorcloths
26 Ledgewood Road
Claremont, NH 03743
(603) 543-0100
www.floorcloths.net
Reproductions of seventeenth- and eighteenth-century floor-cloths

East Knoll North
PO Box 163
Backet, MA 01223
(413) 623-5633
www.eastknollnorth.com
Hand-turned yellowware with banded, feather, and sponge designs

Easton Hill Textile Works
334 Jake Martin Road
Marshfield, VT 05658
(802) 426-3733
Historic reproductions of eighteenth- and nineteenth-century interior fabrics

Elizabeth Eakins Cotton
1 Marshall Street
South Norwalk, CT 06854
(203) 831-9347
Hand-dyed handwoven cotton rugs in traditional patterns

Fioriware
26 North Third Street
Zanesville, OH 43701
(740) 454-7400
www.fioriware.com
Handcrafted yellowware and earthenware using nineteenth-century methods

G. L. Sawyer
2401 Monticello Avenue
Norfolk, VA 23517
(757) 533-9144
Reproduction seventeenth- and eighteenth-century furniture with distressed wood and worn, crackled, milk paint finish

★ Navy "Patriotic Stars with Sawtooth Border" cover-up, from the American Home Collection by Judi Boisson.

★ Copper and brass "Traditional Banner" weather vane, from Wind & Weather.

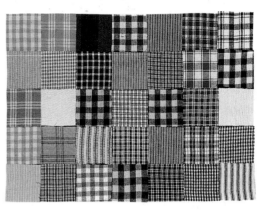

★ Tapestry of handwoven antique reproduction fabrics, from Traditions by Pamela Kline.

Golden Rabbit II
PO Box 188
Arlington, VA 22210
(888) 841-7780
www.spattermatter.com
Cobalt, green, and red swirl enamelware based on eighteenth-century designs

Good Directions, Inc.
20 Commerce Drive
Danbury, CT 06810
(800) 852-3002
www.gooddirections.com
Copper weather vanes, cupolas and accessories in traditional American designs

Hickory Chair
37 Ninth Street Place SE
Hickory, NC 28602
(828) 328-1801
Eighteenth-century reproduction furniture

The Hitchcock Chair Co., Ltd.
31 Industrial Park Road
New Hartford, CT 06057
(860) 738-0141
www.hitchcockchair.com
Handcrafted Hitchcock chairs and Shaker-style furniture

HomArt
920-D Calle Negocio
San Clemente, CA 92673
(888) 346-6278
(949) 366-6240
www.homart.com
Hand-finished lighting fixtures and glassware

Ingersoll Cabinetmakers
Main Street
West Cornwall, CT 06796
(860) 672-6334
ianingersoll.com
Reproduction Shaker-style furniture

Josiah R. Coppersmythe
80 Stiles Road
Boylston, MA 01505
(800) 426-8249
(508) 869-2769
www.jrcoppersmythe.com
Reproductions of early-American lighting fixtures

Lighting by Hammerworks
118 Main Street
Meredith, NH 03253
(603) 279-7352
www.hammerworks.com
Reproduction interior and exterior lighting fixtures and hand-forged door and shutter hardware

Lt. Moses Willard, Inc.
1156 US 50
Milford, OH 45150
(513) 248-5500
Brass, copper, tin, and wooden reproducion lamps and lighting fixtures

Maggie Bonanomi
327 West Walnut Street
Junction City, KS 66441
(785) 762-3477
Handmade baskets in traditional styles

Mason Cash
1901 Route 130
North Brunswick, NJ 08902
(732) 940-8300
www.masoncash.com
Glazed earthenware made in traditional designs

★ Pine drysink in light-blue, from Joseph Spinale Painted Furniture.

★ Sconce in pewter finish, from Josiah R. Coppersmythe.

★ "Pinecone" floorcloth, from Early American Floorcloths.

Palecek
PO Box 225
Richmond, CA 94808
(800) 274-7730
www.palecek.com

Woven-rattan furniture and baskets and metal accessories

Pendleton
PO Box 3030
Portland, OR 97208
(877) 766-4663
www.pendleton-usa.com

Wool reproductions of nineteenth-century blankets

Pennsylvania Firebacks, Inc.
2237 Bethel Road
Lansdale, PA 19446
(888) 349-3002
www.fireback.com

Cast-iron reproduction firebacks

Period Lighting Fixtures
167 River Road
Clarksburg, MA 01247
(413) 664-7141

Reproduction eighteenth- and nineteenth-century lighting fixtures, including Deerfield and Williamsburg collections

Shaker Workshops
PO Box 8001
Ashburnham, MA 01430
(800) 840-9121
www.shakerworkshops.com

Reproduction Shaker furniture and accessories

Joseph Spinale Painted Furniture
79 Linscott Road
Jefferson, ME 04348
(207) 549-7211

Eighteenth- and nineteenth-century-style farmhouse furniture

The Stone House
28 East Market Street
Middleburg, PA 17842
(800) 923-2260

Handcrafted reproduction early American light fixtures.

Thos. Moser Cabinetmakers
27 Wright's Landing
PO Box 1237
Auburn, ME 04211
(800) 708-9703
www.thosmoser.com

Shaker-inspired furniture

Traditions by Pamela Kline
29 Route 9H
Claverack, NY 12513
(518) 851-3975
www.traditionspamela
kline.com

American hand-hooked rugs, reproduction eighteenth- and nineteenth-century hand-woven and printed fabrics; linens and window treatments

Weathervane Hill
1 Testa Place
South Norwalk, CT 06854
(203) 852-4237
www.weathervanehill.com

Handwoven and hand-embroidered fabric

Wind & Weather
1200 N. Main Street
Fort Bragg, CA 95437
(800) 922-9463
www.windandweather.com

Weather vanes, sundials, weather instruments, and garden accessories

Woodard Weave
506 East 74th Street
5th Floor
New York, NY 10021
(800) 332-7847
www.woodardweave.com

Flat-woven rugs and runners in historic American patterns

PROFESSIONAL RESOURCES

We are grateful to the following professionals for allowing their work to be photographed.

ARCHITECTS

Paul Konstant
Konstant Architecture and
  Planning
5300 Golf Road
Skokie, IL 60077
(847) 967-6115
All About Nostalgia
pages 154–159

Susan A. Maxman
Susan Maxman & Partners
1600 Walnut Street
Philadelphia, PA 19103
(215) 985-4410
Born Again
pages 75–79

McKee Patterson
Austin Patterson Diston
  Architects
376 Pequot Ave.
Southport, CT 06490
(203) 255-4031
The Little House that Grew
pages 94–101

Stewart Skolnick
Haver & Skolnick Architects
3 Southbury Road
Roxbury, CT 06783
(860) 354-1031
A Restoration of Character
pages 102–109

Joel Trace
51 Somerstown Road
Ossining, NY 10562
(845) 562-5611
Eclectic Revival
pages 168–173

RESTORATION CONSULTANTS

Jeffrey Morgan
82 Davis Road
South Kent, CT 06785
(860) 937-3028
Guided by Tradition
pages 80–85

Kevin Reiner
PO Box 450
Granville, OH 43023
(740) 587-7098
Rescue Mission
pages 140–145

V. Romanoff Associates
Ithaca, New York
(607) 273-5796
Classical Grace
pages 122–129

DESIGNERS

Larry and Karen Beevers
Kalb Enterprises
Round Top, TX
(979) 249-5015
Lone-Star Landmark
pages 110–117

Lee Bierly and Christopher
  Drake
Bierly-Drake Associates, Inc.
17 Arlington St.
Boston, MA 02116
(617) 247-0081
All About Nostalgia
pages 154–159

Laura Bohn Design
  Associates
30 W. 26th St.
New York, NY 10010
(212) 645-3636
New Rustic Style
pages 132–139

Richard Lear
Lear Design Associates
30 Main Street
Southampton, NY 11968
(631) 283-0272
American Beauty
pages 85–93

DECORATIVE PAINTERS

Virginia Teichner
PO Box 1134
Ridgefield, CT 06877
The Little House that Grew
pages 94–101

ANTIQUES DEALERS

Charles Haver Antiques
3 Southbury Road
Roxbury, CT 06783
(860) 354-1031
A Restoration of Character
pages 102–109

Heidi Johnston
Yellow Monkey Antiques
792 Route 35
Cross River, NY 10518
(914) 763-5848
Eclectic Revival
pages 168–173

LANDSCAPE DESIGNERS

Elizabeth Lear
Lear Design Associates
30 Main Street
Southampton, NY 11968
(631) 283-8649
American Beauty
pages 85–93

Hitch Lyman Garden Design
PO Box 591
Trumansburg, NY 14886
Classical Grace
pages 122–129

Farmhouse Museums

The Farmers' Museum
Lake Road
Cooperstown, NY 13326
(888) 547-1450
www.farmersmuseum.org

A living history farm museum complex that includes a circa 1797 one-and-a-half story wood-frame house with a gable roof.

Fruitlands Farmhouse
Fruitlands Museum
102 Prospect Hill Road
Harvard, MA 01451
(978) 456-3924
www.fruitlands.org

A two-story wood-frame house, circa 1843.

Hans Herr House
1849 Hans Herr Drive
    in Willow Street
Lancaster, PA 17584
(717) 464-4438
www.hansherr.org

A two-story Pennsylvania-German stone farmhouse, circa 1719, with a pitched roof and central chimney.

Abraham Hasbrouk House
Huguenot Historical Society
PO Box 339
New Paltz, NY 12561
(914) 255-1660
www.hvnet.com/museums/
    huguenotst/a_hasb.htm

A stone Hudson Valley Dutch three-room house with a pitched roof, the newest section of which was built in 1712.

★ **Hans Herr House, Lancaster, PA.**

John Johnston Farm
Piqua Historical Area
9845 North Hardin Road
Piqua, OH 45356
(937) 773-2522
www.ohiohistory.org/
    places/piqua

Two-story mixed Dutch Colonial/Georgian-style farmhouse, with furnishings from around 1829.

Lewis-Wagner Farmstead
Winedale Historical Center
Farm Road #2714
Round Top, TX 78954
(979) 278-3530
www.cah.utexas.edu/divisions
    /Winedale.html

Two-story Anglo-American dogtrot farmhouse, circa 1840, with wide porches and Germanic window details and woodwork.

Old World Wisconsin
S103 W37890 Highway 67
Eagle, WI 53119
(262) 594-6300
www.shsw.wisc.edu/sites/oww

A 600-acre museum of farmhouses and outbuildings illustrating the cultural influence of Scandinavian and Eastern-European immigrants.

Landis Valley Museum
2451 Kissel Hill Road
Lancaster, PA 17601
(717) 569-0401
www.landisvalleymuseum.org

A farm museum that includes the Brick Farmstead, a two-and-a-half story brick farmhouse erected in 1815 that has a gabled roof.

Stanley-Whitman House
37 High Street
Farmington, CT 06032
(860) 677-9222
www.stanleywhitman.org

New England saltbox farmhouse, circa 1720.

Adam Thoroughgood House
1636 Parrish Road
Virginia Beach, VA 23455
(757) 460-7588
www.chrysler.org/lightingtour.
    html

Modified hall and parlor house with elements of English cottage architecture, circa 1680.

Christian Waldschmidt House
7567 Glendale-Milford Road
Camp Dennison, OH 45111
(937) 832-4616

Restored 1804 Pennsylvania-German–style home, furnished in the period.

Peter Wentz Farmstead
2100 Schultz Road
Worcester, PA 19490
(215) 584-5104
www.montcopa.org/historic
    sites

Two-story Georgian farmhouse, circa 1758, with Germanic details.

ADDITIONAL READING

Berg, Donald J. **American Country Building Design**. New York: Sterling Publishing Co., 1997.

Butler, Joseph T. **Field Guide to American Antique Furniture**. New York: Owl Books, 1986.

Calloway, Stephen, ed. **The Elements of Style**. New York: Simon & Schuster. Revised Edition, 1996.

Cummings, Abbott Lowell. **The Framed Houses of Massachusetts Bay, 1625-1725**. Cambridge, MA: Harvard University Press, 1979.

Favretti, Rudy J. and Joy P. Favretti. **For Every House & Garden**. Chester, CT: The Pequot Press, 1977.

Gabler, William G. **Death of the Dream: Farmhouses in the Heartland**. Minnesota: Afton Historical Society Press, 1997.

Garrett, Wendell. **American Colonial: Puritan Simplicity to Georgian Grace**. New York: The Monacelli Press, 1995.

_____. **Victorian America: Classical Romanticism to Gilded Opulence**. New York: Rizzoli International Publications, 1993.

Hubka, Thomas C. **Big House, Little House, Back House, Barn: The Connected Farm Buldings of New England**. Hanover, NH: University Press of New England, 1984.

Kahn, Renee and Ellen Meagher. **Preserving Porches**. New York: Henry Holt & Co., 1984, 1990.

Lanier, Gabrielle M. and Bernard L. Herman. **Everyday Architecture of the Mid-Atlantic**. Baltimore: The Johns Hopkins University Press, 1997.

Larkin, David. **The Essential Book of Barns**. New York: Universe Publishing, 1995.

McAlester, Virginia and Lee McAlester. **A Field Guide to American Houses**. New York: Alfred A. Knopf, 1984, 2000.

McMurray, Sally. **Families & Farmhouses in Nineteenth-Century America**. Knoxville: University of Tennessee Press. Revised Edition, 1997.

Schuler, Stanley. **American Barns**. Exton, PA: Schiffer Publishing, 1984.

_____. **Saltbox & Cape Cod Houses**. Exton, PA: Schiffer Publishing, 1988.

Sloane, Eric. **American Barns and Covered Bridges**. New York: Wilfred Funk, Inc., 1954.

_____. **A Reverence for Wood**. New York: Ballantine Books, 1965.

Walker, Lester. **American Shelter**. Woodstock, NY: The Overlook Press, 1981, 1996.

Wilbur, C. Keith. **Home Building and Wood-working in Colonial America**. Guilford, CT: Globe Pequot Press, 1992.

Williams, Henry Lionel and Ottalie K Williams. **Old American Houses and How to Restore Them**. Garden City, NY: Doubleday & Co., 1946.

Wilson, Charles Reagan and William Ferris, eds. **Encyclopedia of Southern Culture**. Chapel Hill: University of North Carolina, 1989.

INDEX

SIMON & SCHUSTER

Rockefeller Center

1230 Avenue of Americas

New York, NY 10020

Copyright ©2002 Smallwood & Stewart, Inc.

Photographs copyright ©2002 by Keith Scott Morton

Manufactured in Hong Kong

10 9 8 7 6 5 4 3 2 1

Library of Congress
Cataloging-in-Publication Data is available

ISBN 0-7432-1929-5

For information regarding special discounts for bulk purchases, please contact Simon & Schuster Special Sales at 1-800-456-6798 or business@simonandschuster.com

All photographs by Keith Scott Morton except:
Michel Arnaud: 133–139; Culver Pictures: 18; Dennis Flaherty: 38–41; Sam Gray: 155–159; the Ferdinand Hamburger, Jr. Archives of the Johns Hopkins University: 39; John Luke: 36–37; Old World Wisconsin: 22–23, 31 top; George Ross: 48; Geoff Spear: 189; Brian Vanden Brink: endpapers, 2–3, 8–11, 13, 14, 19, 21, 24, 25, 27, 28, 30, 32, 34–35, 42, 45 (courtesy Horiuchi & Solien), 47, 50, 51, 52, 54, 57, 190; Jessie Walker: 31 bottom, 33.

Produced by
SMALLWOOD & STEWART, INC. ★ New York

Designed by Amy Henderson

ACKNOWLEDGMENTS

To the homeowners, architects, and designers who opened their farmhouses to us and then graciously spent hours educating me about their history, to Keith Scott Morton whose photography captured the essence of each, and to Amy Henderson for her wonderful and inviting design, I am most grateful.

For so generously sharing their knowledge and resources, I wish to thank: Edward Chappell at the Colonial Williamsburg Foundation; Jeffrey Marshall at the Heritage Conservancy; Eastern Michigan University architectural historian Robert Schweitzer; Jeffrey Morgan, Litchfield County, Connecticut, restoration consultant; historical preservationist George Schoellkopf; Warrie Price, founder of the Conservancy for Historic Battery Park; Diana Salzburg at the Metropolitan Museum of Art; and preservation lecturer Joanne Tuttle, member of the collections committee of SPNEA.

For their unflagging assistance, many thanks to the staff at Smallwood & Stewart, in particular, Paul Blake, Sam Miller, Maria Menechella, and Mary McDonough. Finally, I wish to thank a most supportive, collaborative, and indulgent editor, John Smallwood, without whom this book could not have happened.